The Practice of Self-Management

A handbook for walking the path from reactivity to presence and connection

Christopher Forman
and **Bryan Ungard**

CONSCIOUS
CAPITALISM
PRESS™

Executive editing	*Corey Blake*
Editing	*Geoff Campbell*
	Katherine Catmull
Design and illustration	*Sunny DiMartino*
Letter icons	*Flor Barajas*
Proofreading	*Adam Lawrence*
	Carly Cohen

Conscious Capitalism Press
www.consciouscapitalism.org/press

Round Table Companies
Packaging, production, and distribution services
www.roundtablecompanies.com

Printed in the United States of America

First edition: October 2019
10 9 8 7 6 5 4 3 2 1

Library of Congress Cataloging-in-Publication Data
The practice of self-management: a handbook for walking the path
from reactivity to presence and connection / Christopher Forman
and Bryan Ungard.—1st ed. p. cm.
ISBN paperback: 978-1-950466-05-4
ISBN digital: 978-1-950466-06-1
Library of Congress Control Number: 2019913785

Conscious Capitalism Press is an imprint of Conscious Capitalism, Inc.
The Conscious Capitalism Press logo is a trademark of Conscious
Capitalism, Inc.

Round Table Companies and the RTC logo are trademarks of Writers
of the Round Table, Inc.

Contents

Foreword

Hello, and good wishes! Once you begin to involve yourself with the pages of this book, you'll see that the only way for me to write its foreword is to speak quite directly to you, person to person.

So let me begin by invoking the spirit of Christmas. (Think, for a moment, of Gift, Generosity, Gratitude, and even Glow.) As it happens, I have, on more than one occasion, participated in events planned around the holidays at Decurion, the company led by the authors of this book.

It will certainly be possible for you, or any reader of this book, to derive enormous personal value from engaging it completely on your own, apart from any community of fellow practitioners. But you will better understand both the spirit in which it is being passed on to you, and the difference these practices can make, if you consider that these materials grew up in an organization that quite deliberately invites its members to expand their idea of what it means to "go to work." At Decurion these materials are something of a perpetual Yule Log, bringing light and warmth (and, yes, sometimes heat!) to a work community dedicated to being a space for people to *flourish* (a favorite Decurion word).

At one of these holiday events I overheard a brief but telling conversation between a Decurion employee and Christopher Forman, the company's chairman and owner. Speaking to someone who was probably his boss's boss's boss, this man wanted Chris to know how grateful he was to be working in a place that had helped him become a better version of himself, including a better dad. The words I remember best (I can recall the *sound* of his voice; not just the words) were, "I only hope, in the years ahead, there are more companies like this one, so my kids can have the same kind of experience."

Places like Decurion, and other "deliberately developmental" organizations my colleagues and I have studied and written about, become *gifts* to their constituents through their deep recognition—and honoring of the fact—that *people bring their whole selves to work every day.* We bring our outer activity (what normally gets seen as the totality of "work") *and our inner activity*—the way we are continually making meaning of what we are doing, the way we are managing our thoughts and our emotions.

The materials in this book serve as a foundation for helping people to better engage their interior work—both to improve their outer work and as an end in itself. The authors have at once drawn on the best thinking and practices in human development/transformational learning/personal mastery, *and* used the cumulative experiences of hundreds of their fellow coworkers to polish these stones into something you will want to hold in your hand, something you will not want to let go of.

Merry Christmas!

Robert Kegan

The Meehan Professor of Adult Learning and
Professional Development, Harvard University

Preface

In the late 1990s I looked into meditation. I had long been interested in methods of self-development, both for myself and for the employees of the company I led. And I had read that meditation was effective in spurring a shift from one developmental level to the next.

I read books on insight meditation by people like Jack Kornfield, Joseph Goldstein, and Sharon Salzberg. I liked their approach because it offered the prospect of reducing my knee-jerk reactivity, becoming more present to what was actually happening, and strengthening my connection with other people. More important, the work put an emphasis not on just thinking about these things but on practicing in a way that would bring them about.

I continued to read, adding works in the Advaita Vedanta tradition by Ramana Maharshi, Sri Nisargadatta, and contemporary writers who emphasized the personal experience of self-realization. But my own practice accelerated when I attended a ten-day silent retreat and then, eighteen months later, another silent retreat of seven days, both with Shinzen Young. I now knew exactly what to do when, after leaving these retreats, I sat quietly for twenty minutes every morning. And I found myself becoming less reactive, more present, and more connected with others.

One of the advantages of running a private company is that I get to share—with many other people—ideas and practices I find beneficial, even if they seem odd or unusual. In the early 2000s, meditation was not common in the corporate world. I was tentative in introducing the practices I had learned, at first embedding them in a course on negotiation in order to bolster their business credibility.

I was also not confident enough to develop or teach a course in meditation. At one of the silent retreats I attended, I met Jeremy Hunter, now an associate professor at Claremont's Drucker School of Management. He developed and taught the initial material to several groups of employees. After a couple of years, I decided to take on the teaching myself, adding additional content I found useful. I called the course "The Practice of Self-Management."

Not long afterwards, I invited other employees to become instructors, first teaching alongside me and then on their own. Bryan Ungard, coauthor of this handbook, was one of those instructors, and he and others have now taught the material many more times than I ever did. All told, we have taught the course for more than a decade and a half to hundreds of people. Many of them have returned to the course a second or third time, reporting new insights and value. I also noticed the effects in the company. Groups gained a common awareness, shared language, and personal experience in dealing with reactivity. This gave our people a way to support one another in our practice.

We incorporated some of the course practices into our meetings and other interactions as the company worked on a larger transformation—developing a way of operating that later led to our becoming known as a "deliberately developmental" organization. The course played (and still plays) a central role in the developmental culture we have created among our more than fourteen hundred employees.

A few years ago, seeing the benefits to individuals and for the company, we discussed how to reach more people. This handbook is the result of those many discussions.

How would we recommend you approach this work? Reading this handbook from cover to cover will introduce you to ideas and practices you may find beneficial. But that approach will not result in your getting the greatest possible benefit from the material it contains. The real value will come from diving into and experiencing the book. We focus on practices—meditative practices, daily-life practices, and what we call response practices—and we hope you will take your time with each of them. We recommend that you spend one week on each of the twelve units, engaging in the unit's practices and reflecting on your experiences. Ideally, you will do so with other people: a group at work or a friend or two.

How have we organized the practices? They are in three parts, which we have called Awareness, Understanding, and Transformation. In part 1, we introduce what I learned when I first encountered meditation: how to build my concentration and attention, and then how to direct them to become aware of just how much is constantly going on inside me. People often report that when they begin the first few practices, their minds are flooded with mental images and internal talk, with physical sensations and emotional feelings. What they come to see fairly quickly is that these thoughts, sensations, and emotions were always present but below their level of awareness. Becoming conscious of them allows us to manage them rather than having them manage us.

In part 2, we examine the process that leads to knee-jerk reactions, which we define as automatic behaviors we immediately or later regret. Even before we encounter an external stimulus, we show up with a set of assumptions about how the world is and how it should be, and it's the combination of our assumptions and the external stimulus that can provoke behavior that harms others and contributes to our own suffering. We offer practices to help uncover and examine those assumptions, and we introduce other practices that support being present in the moment to what is actually happening, both externally and internally.

In part 3, we offer meditative and daily-life practices aimed directly at enhancing connection with others, at eliminating the apparent barriers between us. Most of the practices in part 3 were not part of our company's course when first offered, but recent participants report them as among the most powerful. Finally, through a series of response practices, we provide ways of engaging in what is known as skillful speech, a powerful way of bringing us closer to others.

Few of the ideas or practices in this handbook are new. In fact, some of the teachers from whose works we've drawn have altered their approaches in recent years. But we believe that the sequence of practices and the questions for reflection and discussion are uniquely effective in reducing unwanted automatic behavior, increasing the ability to be present, and strengthening connection with others. We have seen this happen for many people over more than fifteen years, and we hope it will be true for you.

Christopher Forman

Invitation

This handbook grew out of our personal experience and the experience of hundreds of employees of the Decurion Corporation, who have spent weeks, months, and even years with the material. The practices it contains rest on the conviction that the more centered, present, and authentic we are as individuals, the more effective we will be in our work and in our lives.

In the work setting, "more effective" might mean communicating with customers and coworkers with authenticity and compassion; meeting difficult issues with an open and curious attitude rather than resistance or procrastination; and getting comfortable with ambiguity and learning anxiety.

The material comes mainly from a course we have taught at Decurion for more than a decade and a half. Our approach includes time-tested practices we have found to cultivate three skill sets.

1. **Being present.** Think about the past few hours. Most likely, you'll see that there were times when you were present, focused, and engaged—perhaps you were reading a good book, cooking a meal, or working on an interesting problem. At other moments, though, your mind drifted, and you weren't fully present to the task or person at hand—or maybe you tried to do several things at once, like talk to your child on the phone while finishing an email. As you've probably noticed, you are a far better professional and human being when you are present and focused. The good news is that you can cultivate this ability to be present.

2. **Reducing reactivity.** Often when you experience an emotion like anger, your feeling takes you over, that is, you become subject to it—under its control—rather than holding your emotion as an object you can observe and manage. When it has you in its grip, you tend to act in ways you immediately or later regret. Reducing your reactivity requires reversing this process. When you can create some distance from your subjective reaction, you can regard even overwhelming feelings with detached gentleness. Then, when a colleague disagrees with you or a customer seems rude,

instead of becoming angry, you can notice the anger arising but not become trapped inside of it. You can notice *Wow, some anger for me there*, the way you might notice a forceful gust of wind.

3. **Dissolving barriers between yourself and others.** Nearly all of us have a habit of erecting defensive barriers between ourselves and the rest of the world. Kindness and compassion help dissolve those barriers. Think of Scrooge at the end of *A Christmas Carol*, when he throws open the window and welcomes in the world.

The practices found in this handbook are not only intended to enhance business effectiveness. Becoming more present, reducing reactivity, and dissolving false barriers between yourself and others will transform your life as a whole. You may find these practices diminish the suffering associated with physical or emotional discomfort and enhance the satisfaction that accompanies physical and emotional pleasure. These results can be captured in two equations:

$$\text{Suffering} = \text{pain} \times \text{resistance}$$

$$\text{Satisfaction} = \text{pleasure} \div \text{clinging}$$

In other words, these practices help you experience physical or emotional pain calmly, without frantically trying to defend yourself, and they allow you to experience pleasure and happiness fully in the moment without the need to cling to your emotional "high." The point of these equations is that when resistance is zero, so is suffering, and eliminating clinging makes satisfaction infinite.

The practices in this handbook may also result in greater consciousness. One is truly conscious when three awarenesses exist:

1. one is aware of one's inner states;

2. one is aware of how one is engaging in the current situation; and

3. one understands how the current situation fits into its larger context.

All three are essential. Purposeful engagement in the world, serving something bigger than oneself, requires letting go of habitual patterns and attachments. And this requires not only good intentions but also deliberate self-development through practices such as those presented in this handbook.

An important note. We present a number of techniques adapted from Eastern spiritual traditions. The Practice of Self-Management is not, however, about religion. As author and philosopher Ken Wilber says, these techniques "are not beliefs, not theories, not ideas, not theologies, and not doctrines. Rather, they are vehicles; they are experiential *practices*. They are experiments to *perform*."[1]

Meditation is one of the main techniques you will use to help yourself become more mindful in all aspects of your life. But the benefits of meditation go far beyond mindfulness: scientists have learned that regular meditation reduces anxiety, enhances sleep, increases relationship satisfaction, improves memory, and enhances executive functions like planning, organizing, and decision-making.

You'll be encouraged to undertake various meditative practices—and we hope you'll continue meditating regularly long after you've completed the Practice of Self-Management program. Aristotle believed that practices—acts performed repeatedly—form habits and that our collection of habits constitutes our character. Hence the importance of practices in becoming the sorts of people we want to be.

What can you expect from this handbook?

1. In part 1, you will encounter the basic concepts of mindfulness and equanimity as well as practices that will help you increase your awareness of your internal states and decrease the number and severity of your knee-jerk reactions.

2. In part 2, you will investigate the Cycle of Reactivity and discover ways to dismantle your default settings.

3. And in part 3, you will explore the power of kindness and compassion to break down barriers that separate you from others, and you'll learn several approaches to skillful communication.

Each of the three parts of this handbook includes several units, and each unit includes two practices: a meditative practice and a daily-life practice. Part 3 also includes several response practices.

You will also find, in each unit, a number of questions. Each provides an opportunity to pause and consider your experiences of the meditative, daily-life, and response practices. They are meant to take you deeper. There are no "right" answers.

Good science involves three steps: the test, the result, and the confirmation of the result. That's what we hope you are going to do with these practices: try them, see what happens, and then compare your experiences with those of others who've tried the practices.

---

1 Ken Wilber, foreword to *Coming Home: The Experience of Enlightenment in Sacred Traditions*, by Lex Hixon (Burdett, NY: Larson Publications, 1995), viii.

You can certainly work through this handbook alone, but we urge you to find friends or coworkers to join you. Try the practices and judge for yourself how using them might make a difference in your life.

To get the most from this handbook and the practices it contains, we recommend you undertake one unit per week over the course of twelve weeks. And again, if it's at all possible, work with another person or a group of people, whether family members, friends, or colleagues. That way, you'll be able to check in with one another, comparing your experiences, and you'll get the most from the discussion questions we've included at the end of each unit.

Reflection Questions

We recommend that you use a journal of some kind to note your responses to the reflection questions that appear in this handbook. Smartphones and computers offer numerous distractions, so consider using paper and pen to record your reflections. We've found over the years that this is far more effective than simply thinking about the questions and moving on. And if you don't have a group to work with, you can still address the discussion questions in your journal.

1. Have you tried meditation or other mindfulness practices before? If so, what was your experience? If not, what do you imagine it will be like?

2. What are your reservations about practicing meditation?

3. What do you hope to gain from mindfulness practice?

4. Do you have a vision of your best and most authentic self? Try to be as detailed as possible in describing this version of yourself and how it differs from your current self.

5. What do you see as your life purpose? What do you think it would take for you to become the person you believe you are meant to be?

6. How do you hope to benefit from the material in this handbook?

Discussion Questions

You've taken time to reflect individually on your initial perceptions of this program and how you hope to develop. Now we recommend you explore some of these questions collectively.

1. What reservations do you have about practicing mindfulness techniques like meditation?

2. What benefits do you expect to experience from practicing mindfulness techniques like meditation?

3. How do you think the people around you (family, friends, coworkers) will benefit from your engagement with this program?

4. You've reflected upon what your best and most authentic self looks like and where you are in relation to that version of you right now. What do you think gets in the way of bridging the gap between your current self and your ideal self?

5. How might you help those around you to become their best and most authentic selves?

Awareness

Introduction

Throughout this program, we'll check in to see whether our practices help you to develop three skills in particular:

Being present (mindfulness)	Reducing reactivity (establishing equanimity)	Dissolving barriers between yourself and others

In part 1, you'll begin a daily practice, and you'll see whether that practice helps you with the first two skills: mindfulness and equanimity.

Mindfulness

Mindfulness is a pillar of this program—but what exactly is it? It might sound abstract and unreal. In fact, though, mindfulness is the opposite of abstraction; it's a full, focused awareness of the reality around and within you.

Imagine standing on a shoreline, watching the waves crest, fall, and crash on the shore. You hear the roar of the surf, smell the briny mix of kelp and seaweed, and feel the wind pelt your skin with sand grit. That moment of deep mindfulness may bring a kind of stillness and clarity—what Zen teacher John Daido Loori calls "finding the still point."[2]

But chances are that as you stand on that beach, your thoughts will drift. Your mindful presence will be hijacked by thoughts of a quarrel with a friend or a work project or what to have for dinner. You are swept away from the beach into an internal narrative: *Who does he think he is? Will my boss see my contribution to our group project? Fish might be nice, but we had shrimp last night . . .*

This kind of internal chatter is perfectly normal. With the practice of mindfulness meditation, you will develop your concentration so that you can return again and again to mindful presence, that inner still point. Mindfulness will make you more aware of and sensitive to your surroundings and the people around you.

Equanimity

Another pillar of our program is non-reactivity, or equanimity—accepting what is without resisting what you dislike or clinging to what you like. You might think of equanimity as a gentle matter-of-factness about what happens around you and what happens inside you, such as your feelings and thoughts.

Equanimity is not an experience but a relationship to experience, one of radical, unconditional non-interference. It involves opening yourself to whatever arises, inside or out.

It is not the same as passivity. It is not to say that if you see something in the world or in yourself that you think needs to be changed, you just ignore it. It is to say you fully accept that things are as they are. From that solid stance, you can be more effective in changing them.

Think of how often in daily life you *don't* experience equanimity.

Say you're late for work, hoping to make that green light—but it turns red before you reach it. A knee-jerk reaction might be to swear or pound the steering wheel, resisting the reality of the red light, wishing it were green.

Or say that you're trying to eat in a healthier way, but someone brings your favorite doughnuts to work, and the scent keeps wafting to your desk. The natural, knee-jerk reaction is to get up and grab a doughnut.

This week, you'll begin the practice of noting your knee-jerk reactions, things you find yourself doing that you immediately or later regret. When you have a knee-jerk reaction, you are not in control. When the doctor taps your knee with his little hammer, it jerks out of reflex. You make no choices about it; the knee rises automatically. Many of your actions in daily life are similar. They occur automatically when provoked by some stimulus.

The good news is that you can regain choice and control. And the first step is simply noticing knee-jerk reactions each time they occur.

---

2 John Daido Loori, *Finding the Still Point: A Beginner's Guide to Zen Meditation* (Boston: Shambhala Publications, 2007).

Practicing noticing—just getting into the habit of becoming aware of your automatic reactions—is the first step. In time, with practice and experimentation, you may find it easier to accept the red light, your desire for doughnuts, or a client's rudeness without judgment or any immediate need to act—in other words, with equanimity. Equanimity gives you the space to respond appropriately, to act in ways you don't later regret.

Expectations

One last word before you jump into the practice. It's easy to get confused or discouraged about the practices and how they're supposed to work. As writer and teacher Ken McLeod has noted, confusion about what you think should happen, what you want to happen, and what actually happens causes many problems in meditation practice. It is helpful to distinguish among an activity's purpose, method, effects, and result.

Think about running. Your *purpose* is to get fit; one *method* is to run regularly. The *effects* will vary from day to day and from person to person. Some days, running might feel great—other days, it's miserable and exhausting. But either way, day by day, the *result* is that strength and endurance are increasing.

Meditation works the same way. Your *purpose* is to acquire the habit of mindful attention and the disposition of equanimity; one *method* is to meditate on the breath. The *effects* will vary: some days, meditation may bring peace and clarity; other days, it may be frustrating and hard. But over time the *result* will be a greater ability to return to mindful presence and equanimity in daily life.

If your meditation sessions are the opposite of peaceful, if there's no "still point" in sight, try to let go of the notion that you're "doing it wrong." The practice is just . . . practice! As long as you're practicing, you're working toward building mindfulness and equanimity. Only by trying can you discover how meditation can work for you.

I Begin to Practice

Introduction

Usually when you practice, you do so with a goal in mind. Before every Major League Baseball game, you'll see the best players in the world on the field hitting, fielding ground balls, and catching fly balls. Or think of piano players—even virtuosos at the top of their profession practice for hours, always looking to improve their world-class skills.

Meditation, though, isn't the same kind of practice. It doesn't have a performance-driven goal. Instead, it has a *purpose*—meditation is the ongoing *practical* testing of certain theories about how our consciousness works. In that way, it is more like a scientific experiment—practicing is about noticing and observing rather than any race to be "best." That is why you don't hear about a Meditation Hall of Fame or an Associated Press Top 25 Meditators.

In fact, you'll find that competitive thinking—*I did it wrong! I have to try harder! Am I good at it yet?*—isn't useful in meditation.

In this section, you'll begin your meditative practice—and you'll quickly see that it requires, well, practice. Ideally, you'll make time to meditate daily—and if not daily, at least several times a week. You'll begin with watching the breath, a fundamental meditative practice that sounds simple but is anything but easy.

To watch your breath, you can count breaths, note the in and out of your breaths, or note the space between your breaths. But whatever practice you adopt, you'll find your attention wanders into thoughts completely unrelated to your breathing.

Whether you suddenly remember you need to make reservations for an anniversary dinner with your spouse, recall a key play in last night's ball game, or find yourself reliving a squabble with a coworker, it is completely normal and human for your mind to wander.

The practice of bringing your attention back to your breath will develop your ability to concentrate and remain present in the moment—the foundation of your ability to develop mindfulness, to find the still point.

Your practice will be to notice that your mind has wandered and then, without judgment, to return your attention to your breath. In some ways, this *is* similar to the mindset of successful baseball players. If they fail to field a ball cleanly, the best players don't throw a tantrum or walk off the field; they simply bring their attention back to the present and prepare for the next play.

Although it is important to meditate without a particular goal in mind, as you continue in your practice, you're likely to notice more quickly when your mind has wandered, and you'll discover you are able to remain focused on your breath for longer periods of time. As your skills develop, you'll begin to apply this growing ability to other objects of attention, like body sensations and emotional states.

Repeatedly noticing when your mind wanders and then returning to your breath is like lifting weights. Eventually, you find you can do more repetitions or lift more weight.

In addition to beginning your meditative practice, you'll adopt a daily-life practice. You will note your knee-jerk reactions—those times when you lean on your horn after another driver darts in front of you, or you get defensive when a loved one questions a decision you've made. The first step in reducing reactivity is to become aware of your knee-jerk reactions, and your daily-life practice will be to note them.

Meditative Practice

Although you could meditate anywhere, some places are better than others. For safety reasons, you wouldn't want to meditate while driving, for example. And for a beginner, a crowded coffee shop, with all its potential for noise and distraction, would be less than ideal.

To begin your practice, find a quiet time and place in your home, office, or even a local park: a time and place when and where you are less likely to be interrupted. If you are not listening to a recording of a meditative practice, we recommend that you set a timer so that you will not have to worry about checking how long you've been sitting or how much longer you have to go. You may want to begin with ten minutes and work your way to longer sessions of, say, twenty-five minutes.

For the meditations in this handbook, we suggest you play a recording so you can focus on the practice instead of trying to read and meditate simultaneously. You can use the version of each meditation that we have prerecorded and made available at www.psm-handbook.com, or you can record yourself reading the meditation aloud. If you elect to listen to the audio on your smartphone, you might set your phone to airplane mode or "Do Not Disturb" each time you begin in order to limit disruptions.

Typically, we picture meditators sitting cross-legged on the floor. If that doesn't sound comfortable or appealing, it's perfectly fine to sit in a chair. If you do, try to keep your back away from the back of the chair and keep your feet flat on the floor. However you decide to sit, keep your spine straight—this will allow you to remain alert yet relaxed.

Consider a smooth stone on the bottom of a clear river. As the water rushes over it, the stone sits. It doesn't need to do anything. Meditation is a lot like being the stone in the water.

With your eyes closed, breathe into your lower abdomen, letting it expand and contract naturally; there is no need to try to control the depth or pace of your breathing. Remember, no effort is required to breathe in. Just allow your breath to take place.

There are a number of ways to focus on the breath. It will be your practice in the beginning simply to count your breaths up to "ten" and then return to "one." When you inhale, count "one." When you exhale, count "two." With each breath, each count, come into the Now. By focusing on your breath, you aren't replaying what happened yesterday or fretting about what might happen later. You are in your breath, feeling the cool air entering, the warm air rushing out. You're practicing being present.

If your mind wanders and you lose track of the count or you find yourself counting "eleven, twelve, thirteen," simply return to "one" and start again. Try to release any judgment you might feel when you find you need to return to "one." Wandering away and then returning to your breath is natural and okay. There are no goals in this practice.

If you find that your mind is wandering a lot—and you're by yourself—try counting aloud. If you find yourself getting sleepy or dull, try straightening your spine. You could also try slightly opening your eyes without focusing on anything; keep a soft gaze, looking through the world rather than at anything directly. Finally, if you find yourself feeling tense, take a deep breath into that tension and relax your body on the out-breath. Pay particular attention to relaxing your shoulders and jaw.

You may find that you're counting to "ten" quite easily without losing count, even though you're also engaging distracting thoughts. If this is the case for you, establish a more demanding threshold for returning to "one." For example, you could return to "one" any time a distracting thought becomes your primary focus and the count becomes more automatic. If you lower your threshold, you may find you're returning to "one" more frequently, and that's okay.

As you become more experienced in your practice, you may want to try returning to "one" any time any thought arises. Remember, thoughts will arise, especially at the beginning of your practice. That's human. Notice your attention has wandered and return your focus to your breath and the count of "one."

Continue to count your breaths for the next few minutes. When you notice your mind has wandered, gently return to "one."

Now, noticing the cool air entering your nostrils and the warm air rushing out, open your eyes.

This practice will develop your concentration and eventually bring you to a state of mindfulness. Each count pulls you to the present moment, to this in-breath, this still point between breaths, this out-breath. The numbers are another name for the present moment, this here, and this Now. With each breath you take, you return to the present.

Remember that the purpose of the practice is not to feel better but rather to fully run the experiment: to notice when your attention has wandered and to bring yourself back to presence. There are days when this practice might result in your feeling refreshed, and there are days when it might leave you feeling depleted. Either is okay.

Meditative Practice Questions

Now that you've started your experimentation, this is a great time to check in with yourself and note how your first experiences with meditation occurred for you. Keep in mind that there are no "correct" answers; if a scientist knew the results before running an experiment, there'd be no need to conduct it. Please also remember that your practice is calling you into a new way of being and thinking. As with any new skill, your results and proficiency will grow with time.

1. What did you notice occurring in your body as you counted breaths?

2. What changes did you notice taking place in your body as you meditated? (For example, did your body feel tense or relaxed at times and in places, or did your body feel tired or more energetic?) Are you aware of the ways you responded to these sensations in your body?

3. How did you feel when you noticed yourself distracted by thoughts? How harsh or kind were you with yourself when you recognized you had become distracted? How did you meet those moments?

4. Think back to the thoughts that arose for you as you tried counting your breaths. What different kinds of thoughts came up for you?

5. Once you've practiced a few days in a row, pay attention to your ability to concentrate and be present outside of your meditation practice and within your daily life. Do you notice any changes there, even small ones? Describe what you notice.

Daily-Life Practice

You stub your toe on a chair leg and flare up into anger. You not only become angry: you may *become anger*, perhaps cursing or yelling at the innocent person nearby, and regretting it later.

Or let's say you notice your neighbor has a fancy new car. If you allow your desire for their car to take hold, you may *become jealousy* and hear yourself making bitter remarks about your neighbor to your spouse as you pull into your driveway. When you think later of the rude things you said about your friendly neighbor, you might feel embarrassment.

You know that when there is no gap between a stimulus and a response, you often find yourself acting in ways you regret, whether immediately or later, after you have calmed down and thought about your behavior. Much of your automatic behavior is positive, and you could certainly not survive if you had to think through every action in advance. We will call the category of automatic behaviors we immediately or later regret "knee-jerk reactions." One way to eliminate these knee-jerk reactions is to gain skill in turning "subject into object," a phrase and approach developed by Harvard professor Robert Kegan to describe how gaining perspective on your feelings can help cut short or prevent this sort of reactivity. Instead of being taken over by anger, becoming subject to that emotion, you can hold the anger as an object in your awareness that is separate from you. When you do so, you empower yourself to shift from "I am angry" to "I notice that some anger is happening." In the former, your anger has dropped you into survival mode and hijacked your ability to reason. In the latter, you give yourself the ability to remain reasonable amidst the intensity of the emotion.

So many situations come up during your day in which you react impulsively or automatically, and in the process, your reaction defines who you are in the moment. At a team meeting, you have an idea about how to solve a problem, but you don't speak up for fear of seeming foolish. Who are you in that moment? Maybe you inadvertently break your mother-in-law's treasured keepsake and then hastily move it behind some books to cover up what you did. Who are you in that moment?

Who are you when a driver runs a red light as you're about to head through the intersection? Who are you when a coworker forgets to compile a report that you need for a meeting in five minutes? Who are you when a neighbor allows his dog to relieve itself in your yard and doesn't clean it up?

In these moments, anger controls most of us: We lean on our horns and shout insults at the driver. We slam our desk or make sharp remarks to our colleague. We shout at our neighbor. In fact, a hallmark of knee-jerk reactions is that they feel *outside of our control*. We didn't mean to finish that whole pint of ice cream or snap at our spouse or waste time when we should have been finishing that report. Perhaps we even actively planned not to do those things. And yet we do them.

Fear and anxiety are normal human emotions. They can, however, lead to impulsive reactions like covering up minor misdeeds, posturing to look good ("Oh yes, of course I've read that book"), fibbing to save face, and freezing up when you know you ought to act. Desire is also perfectly human and normal, but when desire controls you, you might find yourself overeating, shopping compulsively, or flirting when such behavior isn't in service to you. Anger, too, which is often simply a mask of your fear, is normal and human. Yet when anger controls you—when you allow yourself to *become* anger—it can lead you to act in destructive, counterproductive ways that harm others, damage your relationships, and sabotage your own potential. Blowing up at your coworker, after all, will not cause the report to appear or encourage them to meet your future requests enthusiastically.

Of course, understanding the importance of not reacting automatically—of attaining equanimity—is far from achieving it. Many of your reactions are so ingrained that they can take over before you've processed a situation in a conscious way.

If you notice your reactivity, you have a chance to convert the reaction from subject to object, to make it a thing you can observe instead of who you are in the moment.

Your first daily-life practice will be to take note of your knee-jerk reactions—either as they occur or as soon as you have the perspective to recognize them. Keep a list, describing the stimulus that triggered your reaction and then describing your response.

Daily-Life Practice Questions

As your first daily-life practice, you have taken note of your knee-jerk reactions as they occur—or at least as soon as you have the perspective to recognize they have occurred. Caught in the heat of the moment, you are likely discovering that these automatic responses kick in well before you consciously recognize what has happened. As you think about and answer the following questions, refer to your list of knee-jerk reactions.

1. As you noted your knee-jerk reactions, what was your reaction to how often they occurred?

2. Can you see a pattern in what sets off your knee-jerk reactions? What types of situations most often spark your knee-jerk reactions?

3. Can you identify any desired identities or dreaded perceptions by others that seem to threaten your ego and trigger knee-jerk reactions?

4. Although you've only recently started this practice, has noticing your knee-jerk reactions allowed you to step back from them in any way? In other words, have reactions arisen where you've been able to "turn subject to object" and to detach yourself, at least somewhat, from your reaction?

Discussion Questions

In this unit, we've introduced you to two new practices: basic breath meditation and noting knee-jerk reactions. You've had an opportunity to reflect on these practices by yourself. Now we invite you to discuss your experience of them as part of a group, beginning with your experience of meditation.

1. We noted that it was human—and inevitable—that thoughts would intrude on your meditation and might cause you to lose count of your breaths. Was there any pattern you noticed about the types of thoughts that came to you? For example, did you think about work projects? Interpersonal spats? Objects of desire?

2. How difficult was it for you to shed those thoughts and resume your meditation? When thoughts arose, did you find yourself judging yourself—feeling frustration, impatience, or a sense of failure?

3. What differences did you notice in how your body felt during or after meditation?

4. In what ways has your meditation practice affected your ability to concentrate in your daily life?

You also began a daily-life practice of noticing how your thoughts and emotions can prompt knee-jerk reactions—that is, reactions you later regret. Such knee-jerk reactions can take many forms. If you feel jealousy when a coworker gets a promotion you wanted, you may make snide remarks behind that coworker's back. If you're overwhelmed by desire for delicious food, you may overload your plate. If a big project at work scares you, you may distract yourself by saying yes to something easier rather than tackling the project. There are any number of knee-jerk reactions you can experience.

Reflecting now on how you've noticed your knee-jerk reactions, please discuss your observations about this new practice.

1. What patterns did you discover in your knee-jerk reactions?

2. Were you surprised to see how often you respond to situations in a knee-jerk way? Why or why not?

3. Has the practice of noticing your knee-jerk reactions helped you at any point to distance yourself from an overwhelming thought or emotion? Were you ever able to observe a thought or emotion and not let it control you?

This Week's Practices

☐ *Meditative practice—10 to 20 minutes per day:*
Breath meditation.

There are many ways to focus on the breath. It will be your practice in the beginning simply to count your breaths up to "ten" and then return to "one." When you inhale, count "one." When you exhale, count "two." With each breath, each count, come into the now. By focusing on your breath, you aren't replaying what happened yesterday or fretting about what might happen later. You are in your breath, feeling the cool air entering, the warm air rushing out. You're practicing being present.

☐ *Daily-life practice—each day:*
Note knee-jerk reactions.

The first step in reducing reactivity in your life is to notice that it's happening. If you notice your reactivity, you have a chance to convert its causes from subject to object, to make them things you can observe rather than who you are in the moment.

Your first daily-life practice is to take note of your knee-jerk reactions—either as they occur or as soon as you have the perspective to recognize them. Keep a list, describing the stimulus that triggered your reaction and then describing your response.

☐ *Reflection—15 to 30 minutes at the end of the week:*
Choose one or more questions from the Meditative Practice Questions, Daily-Life Practice Questions, or Discussion Questions above, and write about your experience.

I Think

Introduction

In the previous unit, you worked to maintain your focus solely on your breath. When thoughts inevitably arose, because you're human, you nonjudgmentally dropped them and resumed counting your breaths.

This week, you'll experiment with a practice Shinzen Young developed to address the insight that your subjective world is made up of body sensations, mental imagery, and internal talk. The focus for now will be on mental imagery and internal talk—the mental pictures associated with memory, planning, and fantasy, and the running commentary inside your head about yourself, other people, and your circumstances.

Ordinarily, we consider such images and self-talk part of ourselves—part of our *selves*, of who we are. As you began your meditative practice, you focused on the breath, viewing these images and internal dialogue as a distraction to gently set aside.

Now, using one of Shinzen's guided meditations, you'll attempt to make these images and internal talk something you can examine and study—in Kegan's phrase, to "turn subject into object," or turn things you see as part of your very self into things you can distance yourself from and examine. You'll learn to look for your mental screen, the place where you "see" images. You'll also discover your talk home base, the place where you "hear" words and mental rumblings. Later, you'll expand your efforts to study body sensations.

As you develop mindfulness, you'll be able to better understand what is going on in each of these three spheres (mental imagery, internal talk, and body sensations) and become more conscious of how they combine. Greater equanimity will enable you to accept the feelings, images, and internal talk with a gentle matter-of-factness rather than interfere with them by clinging to them or pushing them away. You can then see whether this acceptance empowers you to act in more productive or appropriate ways.

All of this may sound deep, mysterious, and maybe even scary. It's only human to feel discomfort as you begin a new practice. But we'll provide a step-by-step guide to walk you through the process.

As you begin your new meditative practice, you'll also build on your daily-life practice. You'll continue to note your knee-jerk reactions, but now you'll also focus on the images and chatter in your head as you have those reactions.

Remember that you might not feel better when you practice. The purpose of the practice is not to find the still point but to notice and train your attention. There will be days when you feel worse, and that's okay.

Meditative Practice

Today (and, ideally, every day this week) you're going to try a different form of meditation. Instead of focusing on your breath, you'll focus on the sorts of things that actually get in the way of your breath meditation—verbal thoughts and mental images.

As with all the meditations in this handbook, we suggest you play a recording of the meditation so you can focus on the practice instead of trying to read and meditate simultaneously. You can use a version of this meditation that we have prerecorded and made available at www.psm-handbook.com, or you can record yourself reading the meditation aloud.

Just as when you meditated by counting your breaths, your new meditative exercise requires a quiet place in your home, office, or local park, at a time and place you won't be interrupted.

Again, you can sit cross-legged, kneeling, or in a chair. As before, keep your back away from the back of the chair and keep your feet flat on the floor. Sit up straight, alert but relaxed.

Take a deep breath. Now breathe into your lower abdomen, allowing it to expand and contract naturally. There's no need to try to control the depth or pace of your breathing.

As you continue your effortless breathing, close your eyes and rest your attention on what we'll call your image home base or mental screen; this is the place where you "see" mental pictures associated with memories, planning, and fantasy. For most people, that's in front of or behind their eyes. To help locate your mental screen, you can try the POP quiz: is there is a *Person*, *Object*, or *Place* in your consciousness? If so, then there is probably a mental image. Or you can deliberately evoke an image—an apple, say—as a way of locating image home base.

Once you've found your mental screen, take note of any clear or subtle image activity that takes place there. Also, be aware of any clear or subtle image activity that may take place elsewhere, perhaps projected around you or on your body. It's natural if that happens. It's natural if that does not happen.

If you have no image activity, continue to rest your attention on your mental screen. Be aware that it is blank, and enjoy the freedom from the clutter of mental objects.

If your attention wanders into mental talk, body sensations, or external sounds, simply return to your mental screen.

Whether you are aware of clear images, subtle images, or no image activity at all, you are doing this exercise perfectly. That's all you need to do—be aware of the images you have on your mental screen, or be aware that your mental screen is blank.

Once you've done this for a few minutes, you will change your focus. Rest your attention at what we'll call talk home base, the place where you naturally listen for verbal thoughts. To locate talk home base, focus your attention on the spot where you "hear" internal words; for most people, that is right inside their ear canal or somewhere inside their head. One way to find it is to say a word or sentence to yourself and notice where you hear it. Once you've located talk home base, make a note of where it is and keep your attention there. Maintain contact with the verbal component of your thinking process.

At any given moment, verbal thought activity will fall into one of the following mutually exclusive categories:

1. **Clear** words only—a phrase or sentence you could repeat aloud if asked;

2. **Subtle** stirring only—your mental gears are turning, though you may or may not know the theme, and it's not possible for you to repeat exact phrases or sentences;

3. Dead **silence** only; or

4. **Clear** words with a simultaneous undercurrent of **subtle** activity.

Remaining focused on talk home base, listen to the activity there in terms of the four states. Listen restfully. You don't need to intentionally label the activity.

Now, if there are **clear** words, listen to them as *sounds*.

If there is **subtle** stirring, let it move as it wishes.

If there is **silence**, actually hear the silence.

Or, if there is a **mix of clear and subtle**, listen to the sound of the clear words and let the subtle ones stir.

If you find yourself pulled away from talk home base by external noises, physical sensations, or emotional feelings, simply return to talk home base. Don't judge yourself for being distracted. You're human, and it's natural to lose focus. Simply return to talk home base as soon as you realize you've drifted.

Now, return to your breath. Feel the cool air come in, the warm air rush out. With each breath, return to the present, to the Now.

Open your eyes.

Meditative Practice Questions

In this unit, we switched gears on you. Instead of telling you to let go of the thoughts and images you had while meditating, we asked you to dwell on them—but as objects to examine, not as vehicles to be swept away by. Although simple in theory, the practice itself—like your breath meditation—can be more difficult than it sounds. The key is not to fret about whether you're doing it right. As with any of your practices, the perfection is in the doing. Here are some questions to help you reflect on your experience:

1. Were you able to locate your image home base or mental screen? If so, where was it?

2. If you were aware of clear or subtle images, what did you see? If your mental screen was blank, what did it look like?

3. Did you notice any clear or subtle image activity elsewhere, perhaps projected around you or on your body? If so, where was it and what did you see?

4. Were you able to locate your talk home base? If so, where was it?

5. We noted that verbal thought activity could take the form of clear words, subtle stirring, silence, or clear words with simultaneous subtle stirring. What type of verbal thought activity did you hear? Was there a pattern to the subjects of your verbal thought activity?

6. Did you find it easier or harder to focus on your image or talk home base than it was to focus on your breath? Why do you think that is?

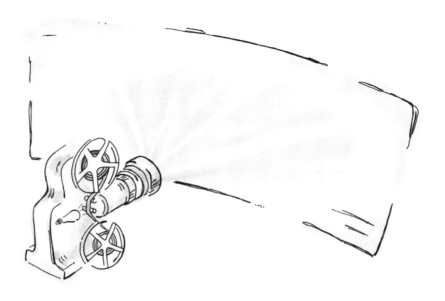

Daily-Life Practice

By now, you've probably noticed that you have knee-jerk reactions to a variety of stimuli throughout the day. You may even be surprised to see how much of your life appears to be ruled by impulses you act on without even thinking, immediately or later regretting your actions.

Now we'd like to take that general awareness you're developing and invite in more detail. For your daily-life practice, you'll continue to keep track of your knee-jerk reactions. But now you'll focus on how those knee-jerk reactions manifest in your internal space. What words and rumblings of thoughts do you hear in your head? What images appear on your internal screen?

Perhaps you have a presentation to give three days from now. Every time you see that file on your computer, you hear words in your head along the lines of, *Oh no. I'm not prepared. I'm terrible at these things.* Perhaps on your mental screen you see yourself standing in front of a roomful of people, stumbling and stammering, while they fidget and your boss glares.

Or maybe you walk past a pizza parlor and catch a deep whiff of baking pies. On your mental screen, you might see a piece of your favorite pizza, melted cheese pulling away from the slice, and you dart inside to buy a slice even though you're not hungry and you're trying to watch your carbohydrates intake.

Maybe you open an email from your supervisor thanking you for applying for a new job, adding that she regrets to inform you that the position is going to someone else. You notice lots of fuzzy image activity, or maybe you hear clear words mixed with a torrent of subtle verbal thought activity. *Jerk*, you might think, or *I'm a failure*, along with a buzz of other words you can't quite make out.

The daily-life practice for this unit is to note knee-jerk reactions as they occur or soon after, and to be aware of the mental images and internal talk that accompany them. We suggest making notes in your journal.

Daily-Life Practice Questions

Sometimes it's something that makes us happy. Sometimes it's something that makes us mad. Or envious. Or even confused. But throughout each day, things happen, and we find ourselves reacting without thinking.

You began by taking note of these knee-jerk reactions, and now you're collecting additional data about them. In this section, we asked you to note the verbal thought activity and the imagery on your mental screen when you find yourself having a knee-jerk reaction.

Please think about and answer the following questions.

1. Did you hear more internal words or see more mental images during your knee-jerk reactions? Which was more vivid for you and in what ways?

2. When you saw mental images, did they tend to take place on your image home base—your mental screen—or did you find they were more often projected around you or on your body?

3. When you had verbal thought activity, did you tend to "hear" clear words, subtle stirring, or some combination of the two?

4. Did you notice whether certain types of stimuli tended to provoke inner talk while others tended to trigger mental imagery? For example, did you find that when you were angry, you heard words, but when you desired something, you saw images?

5. Did you notice whether one type of inner response—either talk or images— reinforced your behavior? In other words, if you heard words when angry, were you more likely to exhibit angry behavior? If you saw images when feeling desire, were you more likely to try to satisfy that desire?

Discussion Questions

In this unit, we introduced a new practice: you meditated on what appears on your mental screen and the activity in your talk home base. You've had an opportunity to reflect on your experience with this kind of meditation. Now please discuss as a group your observations about this new practice.

1. In what ways did trying to focus on mental chatter as "objects" help you quiet that chatter? In what ways did it intensify the mental self-talk?

2. Likewise, in what ways did focusing on your mental screen help you detach from the images there? In what ways did it make them more vivid?

3. When you focused on talk home base and heard clear words, what was it like for you to listen to them as sounds? If you instead felt a subtle stirring, what was it like to let it move as it wished? If you heard silence, what was it like for you to hear that silence?

You also incorporated this new focus into your daily practice, observing the words and images in your head when you experience knee-jerk reactions. Reflecting now on your experience with noting your imagery and self-talk during knee-jerk reactions, please consider the following questions.

1. During a knee-jerk reaction, did you find that your words and/or images were especially vivid? Or were they more general and less tangible?

2. Did you notice a pattern to your mental activity during knee-jerk reactions? In other words, were you more likely to hear words or see images while reacting?

3. Did the process of observing your self-talk and your images help you to step back from your reaction and allow you to consciously respond in a different, perhaps more positive, way?

This Week's Practices

☐ *Meditative practice—10 to 20 minutes per day:*
Note mental imagery and internal talk.

For this week, you'll experiment with a portion of what Shinzen Young considers core practice, based on the insight that your subjective world is made up of body sensations, mental imagery, and internal talk. You'll focus for now on mental imagery and internal talk—the mental pictures associated with memory, planning, and fantasy and the running commentary inside your head about yourself, other people, and your circumstances.

☐ *Daily-life practice—each day:*
Note knee-jerk reactions, with a focus on mental imagery and internal talk.

For your daily-life practice, you'll continue to keep track of your knee-jerk reactions. But now you'll focus on how those knee-jerk reactions manifest in your internal space. What words and rumblings of thoughts do you hear in your head? What images appear on your internal screen?

☐ *Reflection—15 to 30 minutes at the end of the week:*
Choose one or more questions from the Meditative Practice Questions, Daily-Life Practice Questions, or Discussion Questions above, and write about your experience.

I Feel

Introduction

Notice a body sensation you are experiencing right now. Focus on it, just for a moment.

What do you notice? It may be a purely physical sensation—cool air on your arm or stiffness in your neck.

Or it may be a sensation connected to an emotion. That's not surprising because the two types of sensation are often intertwined. Think about a time when you were unprepared for a meeting. You may have felt fear, and you may have noticed your stomach tighten and your pulse quicken. The sensations may have been so strong you felt paralyzed and unable to do anything more to prepare.

Sensations can be broken into two types.

Purely *physical* sensations are one type, and many times they can take over our thinking. That's hardly surprising; scientists estimate the human body contains ninety-five to one hundred billion neurons, or nerve cells. Think of the way your skin feels when the wind blows against you, or recall the aches and pains you feel following a hard workout. Your stimulated neurons call for your attention.

The other type of body sensations we can experience are *feelings*—emotional states like anxiety or irritation, which we might experience when we get asked to do something we've never done before; or joy when we see puppies wrestling in the park.

By focusing on body sensations, we hope to see whether we can study them instead of getting stuck in them or ruled by them.

In this unit, you'll focus on body sensations, both physical and emotional. Likewise, you'll tweak your daily-life practice. You'll continue to note your knee-jerk reactions, but you'll pay special attention to the body sensations that come up during them.

For example, after being cut off in traffic, perhaps you'll note an increase in your heart rate and detect anger in other parts of your body. Or maybe you'll receive a letter from the Internal Revenue Service, feel your stomach tighten, and note fear.

After you've had time with the practice, we'll ask you some questions to see what you discovered.

Meditative Practice

When we think of flavor, we tend to think of our sense of taste. Is this food salty? Sweet? Bitter? Sour? Umami? Go to an ice-cream parlor, and your big decision will be what flavor— or flavors—of ice cream to enjoy.

In this week's meditation, again taken from the work of Shinzen Young, we use the word "flavor" in a broader way. He introduces the idea of exploring the "flavors" of sensation that arise in the body. We'll refer to physiological sensations as "touch flavors" and emotional sensations as "feel flavors."

Touch flavors are physical body sensations. Think about a time when you sat clasping your hands gently. What body sensations did you experience as your hands touched? Those are touch flavors. Feel flavors involve emotions like anger, fear, joy, or interest and are often present in both the body and the mind.

Like any other form of meditation, meditating on body sensations requires concentration and practice; you'll get more skilled in noting touch and feel flavors by doing this meditation more than once during the week.

As always, we suggest you play a recording of the meditation so you can focus on the practice instead of trying to read and meditate simultaneously. You can use a version of this meditation that we have prerecorded and made available at www.psm-handbook.com, or you can record yourself reading the meditation aloud.

Find a position that allows you to stay sharp—alert yet reposed. For most people, this will involve sitting. But if you're feeling sleepy or fuzzy, it's okay to stand in place.

Begin by taking a deep breath, allowing your gaze to soften. Take a moment to stretch up and settle in. Closing your eyes, take another deep breath, feeling the breath enter and leave you. Allow your breath to become natural again.

Now bring your awareness to sensations associated with your posture. If you're not sitting up or standing up straight, you may notice a tightness in your back or neck, for example. There is no need to change anything; just be aware.

Next, bring awareness to sensations associated with gentle touches. Perhaps you note the sensations of your seat cushion, or the way your clothes are draped on your body. Perhaps you note the sensation of one of your hands resting in the other. Maybe you feel a gentle breeze on your face from a ceiling fan or the air conditioner.

After you've identified sensations associated with gentle touches, bring your awareness to physical sensations associated with your breathing. Here, you may note the feel of the air entering your nostrils, for example, or a feeling of fullness in your lungs.

Now bring awareness to your circulation and the beating of your heart. Depending on your body and your level of relaxation and concentration, you may feel your heartbeat in your pulse points.

Next, bring your awareness to sensations associated with the state of your bladder. If it's full, you'll notice a familiar discomfort, often projected elsewhere in your body.

Now bring your awareness to your stomach and bowel. Do you feel a rumbling? A fullness?

Shift your awareness to your general body state: are you alert or sleepy, filled with energy or tired?

Bring your awareness to sensations associated with special states of the body. Do you have aches and pains from a recent workout? Do you have an itch? Does your body ache because you're coming down with a cold?

Finally, let your awareness of touch flavors float freely. As you note different touch sensations, try labeling them: posture, gentle touches, breathing, circulation, bladder, bowel, aches. Maybe you are aware of your breathing, so you'll mentally say, "breathing," or you note the feel of your shirtsleeve on your arm, so you say to yourself, "gentle touch." Stay with each sensation for a few seconds. Soak into it. And then note the next one that arises in your awareness.

Some of the other things we've worked with or mentioned—like mental images, internal talk, and emotions—may also arise, of course. For now, just let those float away, and focus on touch.

Let the touch flavors come to you—there is no need to chase after them. Likewise, let go of the desire to try to figure things out—there is no need to question why your breathing is shallow, for example, or why your back is tensing. Simply label that these things are. Stay with each flavor for two or three seconds.

You may have a clear awareness of more than one flavor at a time. You might note "pain and circulation" or "breath and posture," for example.

Now, staying with the body, we'll shift from touch flavors to feeling flavors. For most people, these tend to arise along the central axis of the body, including the forehead, brow, eyes, lips, jaw, throat, chest, heart, diaphragm, and abdomen—areas we might call the "feeling centers."

At any given instant, you may have just one feeling or emotion present. It may be subtle. If you have one emotional flavor present, label it with the most general or generic label you're comfortable with. Common labels on the uncomfortable side include "anger," "fear," "sadness," "embarrassment," "impatience," and "disgust." Common labels on the pleasant side include "joy," "interest," "humor," "peace," "love," and "gratitude." Of course, there are more, but these are among the most common.

If you have more than one emotion present, label them with the conjunction *and*. So you might detect "fear and sadness," for example, or "fear and interest." If you find additional flavors, label them as well, using the conjunction "and."

There are only four possible feeling states. At any given time, you may experience:

1. A single emotional feeling, such as joy; OR

2. Two or more feelings at the same time: "fear and anger," for example; OR

3. A subtle mixture in which you are not able to discern individual qualities, but you can still tell several are mixed; OR

4. No feelings at all; complete emotional neutrality.

Noting which state you are currently experiencing and labeling any feelings that arise can help you gain insight into what you are feeling, which may turn out to be quite different from what you would have expected. As you label, it's okay to guess.

Although there are many possible emotional flavors, you'll probably find that only a few basic ones come up for you. These are probably the qualities that rule your behavior. There are several ways you might become aware of your feelings. Here's what to do in each case.

If you become aware of the emotion through your body alone: focus on that body sensation for a few seconds. Bring your mindfulness and equanimity to bear, as well as a sensitivity to change. Then move on to the next feeling that arises.

If the emotion feels present primarily in your mind: then bring your focus back to the body to see whether you detect a physical sensation as well. Did that thought or image bring about something in your body? If there is a body sensation, focus on it, and bring to bear your mindfulness, equanimity, and a sensitivity to change. If there is no body sensation, that's okay, too. Just go on to label the next emotional flavor you notice.

If you've become aware of the emotion through both your mind and body: focus on your body. Bring to bear your mindfulness, equanimity, and a sensitivity to change to the feeling. Then move on to the next feeling.

As you continue during the next few minutes, you'll likely discover a natural rhythm for labeling. Your labels may sound like, "fear . . . anger . . . interest . . . humor . . . fear and interest . . . none . . . subtle . . . interest and humor . . . none . . . none . . . impatience." As a general rule, labeling every second is too fast, but labeling every five seconds is probably too slow. If you're by yourself, you can label aloud. Otherwise, just do internal labeling, that is, say the labels to yourself.

Remember, it's okay to guess. And as with our other forms of meditation, try to relax your desire to analyze why you have a feeling or to try to figure it out. Just note it and let it *be*.

Now, let go of labeling. For the next few minutes, focus on staying in simple contact with your feeling centers.

Now, take a deep breath, feeling the cool air come in and the warm air rush out. Take another deep breath, this time opening your eyes.

Meditative Practice Questions

In this unit, you shifted your meditation focus from mental imagery and internal talk to body sensations, both physiological and emotional. Some of the things you noticed during the first part of the meditative practice were probably familiar to you—a numbness or discomfort after sitting in one place for a while, for example—while others may have been entirely new to you. How often, after all, do you reflect on the sensation of your shirt resting on your skin? Below are some questions to help you to think about your experience of meditating on body sensations by noting touch flavors.

1. In your noticing, what surprised you? In noting touch flavors, what sensations did you notice that you would ordinarily overlook or dismiss?

2. During your meditation, what sensations did you notice changing from one extreme to another? For example, did you feel alert at some points and sleepy at others?

3. As you were experiencing certain body sensations, were you able to simply remain present with them, or did your mind attempt to make meaning from them? Was it easy or hard to leave those thoughts behind?

4. During the part of the guided meditation in which you were asked to let your awareness freely float in touch, you were instructed to let the flavors come to you. When you did that, which touch flavors came to you more quickly or clearly than others?

5. Were you ever clearly aware of more than one touch flavor at a time? If so, what were they?

During the second part of the meditative practice, you mentally labeled your feeling qualities, whether single, compound, subtly present, or completely absent. Reflecting on your experience of noting your feeling flavors, please consider and answer the following questions.

1. As you began your meditation on feeling flavors, you were encouraged to focus on your feeling centers. Which feeling center was most active for you? Were certain centers associated with certain feeling flavors?

2. In labeling your feeling flavors, did you most often find yourself feeling more than one flavor or one at a time?

3. Were most of your feelings on the pleasant side (joy and peace, for example) or uncomfortable (like fear or disgust)?

4. What surprised you about how active and varied your feeling states can be?

Daily-Life Practice

As part of your daily practice, you've continued to focus on noting your knee-jerk reactions. Now you're building on your awareness about what is happening *inside you* during these episodes. You recently began taking note of the internal dialogue and mental images you have during your knee-jerk reactions. Now, we'd like to shift your daily-life practice to an awareness of what happens in your body both physically and emotionally during those reactions.

Maybe, when asked to give a presentation to one hundred colleagues, your stomach tightens, your mouth gets dry, and you immediately offer an excuse for not being able to do so. You note fear and anxiety.

Maybe you see someone you barked at the day before, and your face flushes while your heart races as you duck into an empty office. You pause for a moment and note fear and anger.

Just as when you took note of the words, rumblings of thoughts, and internal screen images during knee-jerk reactions, you'll be noting your body sensations to see whether you can study them instead of being ruled by them.

The daily-life practice for this week is to note knee-jerk reactions (make a list as they occur) and also to note what happens in your body, both physically and emotionally, when you fall into them.

Daily-Life Practice Questions

By now you've come to see how much of your life is ruled by knee-jerk reactions. You began by simply noting your knee-jerk reactions, and then you took stock of the internal dialogue and mental images you have during these episodes.

Now you're examining the body sensations you experience during knee-jerk reactions. Please consider and answer the following questions about how noticing those sensations has occurred for you.

1. Which part of your body has seemed particularly active during knee-jerk reactions? Has the answer to that question depended on what type of incident you were reacting to?

2. When did you experience similar physical reactions to dissimilar events? For example, did your heart race both when you reacted angrily to an event and when you reacted with pleasure to something?

3. Which specific physical reactions tended to coincide with certain emotional feelings?

4. How close a connection was there between what you were feeling emotionally and what you felt in your body during knee-jerk reactions?

5. Reflect on your most intense knee-jerk reaction. What was happening in your body during that time? Since you've started noting your knee-jerk reactions generally and some of the things happening within your body specifically, have the number and intensity of your reactions increased or have they seemed to diminish?

Discussion Questions

In this unit, you shifted your focus to body sensations. Reflecting on your meditation experience with physiological and emotional sensations, consider and answer the following questions as a group:

1. What surprised you about how much is going on in your body at any given time?

2. What surprised you about how much your emotional state fluctuated from moment to moment?

3. Where in your body did you feel specific emotions?

4. Where did you first detect the majority of your feelings—in your body or in your mind?

5. What are you learning from observing your body sensations?

Just as you focused on body sensations during your meditation practice, you also examined, as part of your daily-life practice, the physiological and emotional flavors that arose during knee-jerk reactions. To help you reflect on your experience with this practice, please discuss your thoughts about the following questions as a group:

1. Describe the relationship between your body sensations and your knee-jerk reactions. Did one seem to cause the other? Did they arise together? In what ways did they intensify each other?

2. What patterns in your body sensations did you notice during your knee-jerk reactions? In other words, did you tend to notice one type of physiological or emotional reaction above all others?

3. Did noticing body sensations during a knee-jerk reaction help you to pull back from that reaction? Did it help you turn the sensations and feelings from subject (*I'm anxious!*) to object (*Ah, some anxiety is happening*)?

This Week's Practices

☐ *Meditative practice—10 to 20 minutes per day:*
Note body sensations. Use the meditative practice to explore the "flavors" of sensation that arise in the body, both physiological and emotional.

☐ *Daily-life practice—each day:*
The daily-life practice for this week is to note knee-jerk reactions with a focus on body sensations, both physiological and emotional. Make a list of the reactions as they occur, and also note what body sensations triggered or accompanied each reaction.

☐ *Reflection—15 to 30 minutes at the end of the week:*
Choose one or more questions from the Meditative Practice Questions, Daily-Life Practice Questions, or Discussion Questions above, and write about your experience.

I Notice

Introduction

You're watching what you eat, but as you pass a barbecue joint, you catch a whiff of roasting pork. You see a thick pulled-pork sandwich in your mind's eye, and you hear the words *I'm so hungry* in your inner ear. Your stomach growls and your mouth waters. Then you sense an emotion—desire—along with some more subtle emotional flavors swirling around as well: perhaps guilt (*I shouldn't*), perhaps anger (*Well, why can't I eat? I'm hungry!*), perhaps joy (*It's exactly what I want!*).

For the past two weeks, you've looked at your interior life, section by section. You started with mental imagery and internal chatter, and you moved to physical sensations and emotions.

This week, you'll bring it all together. You'll take the images, self-talk, physical sensations, and emotions and examine them. In the words of this program, you'll take these things you are normally *subject to* and turn them into something you can look at: *object*.

In the process of developing mindfulness, you'll become more precisely aware of what is going on in each of these areas of your interior life and more conscious of how they combine to fuel your behavior.

As a pressing deadline nears and you fear you won't meet it, you keep seeing images of your supervisor being disappointed with you. *I've got to finish. I can't be a failure!* you think. Your stomach tightens, and your heart races. *I can't let everyone down! I was late on a project just last month—if it happens again . . .* Now you feel fear, and you can hardly focus on your work.

Look at what's happening here. That panicky self-talk: is that how you would talk to a worried friend in this situation? Of course not, because you'd have enough distance to see that it would be neither useful nor compassionate. That racing heart: can you tell that it is fueling the panicked words while also beating all the faster because of them? That image you've painted of a disappointed supervisor: no wonder your stomach feels sick. Physical sensations, images, feelings, and self-talk have fused together, multiplying their force. Your whole organism has become like the "Don't Panic" moment in the movie *Airplane!* in which passengers run up and down the aisle frightening one another out of their wits.

Feelings, physical sensations, self-talk, self-painted images—all of these can rile each other up to a boiling point. But mindfulness can interrupt this cycle. By learning to notice each element as it arises—the words and pictures, the physical sensations and emotional feelings—and then teasing them apart and observing them separately, you diminish their intensity. They no longer have the power to control you.

As you develop increasing equanimity, you'll have a greater ability to accept these things gently rather than interfere with them by clinging to them or pushing them away.

You will also expand your daily-life practice. While continuing to monitor your knee-jerk reactions, you'll broaden your focus to look at body sensations and feelings, the words and rumblings you hear in your head, and the images that appear in your mind during these episodes.

Meditative Practice

This week you'll use a practice from Shinzen Young to put together what you've done separately over the past several weeks—focusing first on your body, through an examination of physical sensations and emotions, then on your mental images, continuing through your self-talk, and then finishing by freely floating through your interior space.

You'll need to find a quiet place where you can be uninterrupted for ten, twenty, or even thirty minutes.

As always, we suggest you play a recording of the meditation so you can focus on the practice instead of trying to read and meditate simultaneously. You can use a version of this meditation that we have prerecorded and made available at www.psm-handbook.com, or you can record yourself reading the meditation aloud.

Find a comfortable position that allows you to be alert. For most people, that will mean sitting. If you find yourself getting sleepy or dull during this practice, try straightening your spine or opening your eyes, looking through the world rather than at it. Or you could stand up. If you find your muscles tensing, try taking a deep breath and relaxing your shoulders on the out-breath.

To begin, take a deep breath, feeling the cool air come in through your nostrils and warm air rushing out through your mouth. Take another deep breath, this time closing your eyes on the in-breath.

Breathing normally, bring your attention to your settling body. Try to establish simple contact with your body sensations. By simple contact, we mean only that you are continuously aware of something somewhere in your body. Sensations in your body can be physical, like a pain in your shoulder or an itch on your leg, or emotional, like a feeling of sadness or peace.

There is no need to intentionally try to note things like flavor, location, or shape. If that happens for you spontaneously, that is okay. But simple contact is a low-effort practice, and we keep conceptualizing to a minimum.

Locate a physical sensation somewhere in your body.

Locate an emotional feeling somewhere in your body.

Note if your body sensations are obvious, concrete, and intense, or if they are subtle and cloudy, like a whisper in a crowded room.

Note if your body sensations are localized with definite boundaries, or if they are widespread, possibly extending beyond what you consider the boundaries of your physical body.

Note if your attention is staying in one location or if it is moving around, or if it is divided between two or more locations.

If at any time you find yourself distracted by outside sounds, internal talk, or mental images, simply return your attention to your body as soon as you notice the distraction.

Continue to survey your body for sensations for the next minute or so.

Now, turn your attention to your image home base. It might be in front of or behind your eyes. If there is a person, object, or place in your consciousness, wherever you see that image is your mental screen.

Note any clear or subtle image activity taking place on your mental screen. If you have no images, remain aware of your mental screen's blankness, and enjoy your freedom from mental clutter.

Now, check to see whether you have any clear or subtle image activity outside your mental screen. Perhaps something is projected near you or on your body.

If you find your attention wanders into mental talk, body sensations, or something else, just return your focus to your mental screen as soon as you notice you've wandered.

Whether you're aware of any clear or subtle images anywhere, or you're aware that you have no image activity at all, you are doing this exactly right. Remain aware of the activity—or lack of it—on your mental screen. That is all you have to do.

Take another minute to continue focusing on your image home base.

Now, shift your focus to talk home base, the place where you naturally listen for verbal thoughts. Place your awareness in your ear canals and listen into your head for mental words. Keep your focus on wherever you hear the words; for most people, it's inside the ear canal or somewhere inside the head.

Note where talk home base occurs for you.

Rest your attention at talk home base and listen to the activity.

Note which activity is clear—a phrase or sentence you could repeat aloud.

Note which activity is subtle stirring—where you can hear it but cannot quite make out distinct words.

Note which activity is clear words with an undercurrent of subtle stirring.

Finally, note when you experience silence.

Notice the difference in each kind of activity.

As you continue to rest your attention on talk home base, try to listen to clear words as sounds rather than focusing on their meaning. If you note a subtle stirring, allow it to move as it wishes. If there is silence, hear the silence. And if there is a mix of clear and subtle, listen to the sound of the clear words and let the subtle ones stir.

If you find you've left talk home base, just return to it as soon as you notice.

Continue to listen to your self-talk—or silence—for the next minute or so.

Now let go of talk home base and allow your awareness to float freely among your body sensations, mental imagery, and internal talk.

You might notice physical or emotional sensations in your body. You might notice mental images. You might notice internal talk. You might notice combinations of body and image, body and talk, image and talk, or body and image and talk. You might notice the absence of all of these.

There are exactly eight different states you can note. There may be only sensations (physical or emotional) in the body. There may be only mental images. There may be only internal talk. You may experience combinations of two of the three (body and image, body and talk, image and talk) or of all three at once (body, image, and talk). And all may be absent, in which case you would note "none." Let your attention go where it wants, floating freely.

Now, for the next few minutes, note with verbal labels (either to yourself or out loud) which of the eight possible states is occurring. Labeling every second is probably too fast, every five seconds, too slow. As you say the labels, either to yourself or aloud, use a gentle, matter-of-fact tone. This can contribute to equanimity. And, by the way, there's no need to label the labels, so you don't need to say "talk" every time you label.

Again, the eight possible labels are:

"Body."

"Image."

"Talk."

"Body and image."

"Body and talk."

"Image and talk."

"Body and image and talk."

"None."

Try to label every few seconds.

Use a gentle, matter-of-fact tone.

As we conclude this meditation, free-float for a minute or so without labeling.

Now bring your attention back to your breath. Feel the cool air come in through your nose and the warmth of the breath on your exhalation. Take another deep breath and open your eyes.

Meditative Practice Questions

In this unit you synthesized components of your recent practice, noting and labeling everything that was happening within your body and mind. Reflecting upon your experience, please consider and answer the following questions.

1. What surprised you about how much goes on in your interior space at any given time?

2. What connections did you notice among your internal talk, mental images, emotions, and body sensations?

3. In what ways did watching (rather than surrendering to and identifying with) your internal talk, mental images, emotions, and body sensations dull their intensity or make them more intense?

4. You watched your internal talk, mental images, emotions, and body sensations. Was one of those categories more active than the others?

5. In what ways are you finding it easier to keep your focus during meditation?

Daily-Life Practice

You're in the middle of a presentation when you realize you're missing a page of notes. At first you flip frantically through the binder, once, twice, feeling all eyes on you. Your heart is racing uncontrollably, so hard you can feel it beating in your ears. You feel fear and embarrassment. *You're blowing this in front of your boss*, your internal talk says. Even though you're still staring at the floor, on your mental screen you see discomfort and disappointment written on the faces of everyone in the room. How might the techniques we've been practicing—noticing your self-talk and images, your physical sensations and feelings—help you in this moment?

In the last unit, you continued the practice of noting your knee-jerk reactions, with a focus on your body sensations, both physiological and emotional. Previously you focused on mental imagery and internal talk.

Now you will bring all those practices together. This unit's daily-life practice is to continue to note your knee-jerk reactions with a focus on everything happening within your interior space during these episodes: physical sensations, emotions, mental imagery, and internal talk. Keep a list of the reactions (behaviors you immediately or later regret) with notes on what was happening in your interior space.

Daily-Life Practice Questions

This week, you've continued your practice of noting your knee-jerk reactions—with a special focus on all that happens within your interior space when you're having them. During the last few weeks, you've taken a systematic approach, looking separately at what happens with your inner talk, mental images, physical body, and emotions. This week, you put it all together.

Reflecting upon your experience with this practice, please consider and answer the following questions.

1. What types of situations provoked your most intense knee-jerk reactions?

2. Which part of your interior space tended to be most activated during a knee-jerk reaction?

3. How did the separate components of your interior space intensify one another during a knee-jerk reaction?

4. How did noting your knee-jerk reactions and monitoring what was happening in your interior space tend to intensify or reduce the strength of your reaction?

5. What has been the change in the number and intensity of your knee-jerk reactions since you started noting them?

Discussion Questions

In this unit, you took a panoramic look at what happens within your body and mind—a big-picture perspective of what takes place in your internal talk, mental screen, physical body, and emotional life. You've had an opportunity to reflect individually upon this experience through a series of questions. Now we invite you to reflect as a group by considering and answering the following questions.

1. In what ways were you surprised to observe how much happens within your interior landscape at any given time?

2. What did you notice about the interconnectedness between what was happening with your internal talk, mental screen, physical body, and emotions?

3. When you reached the free-float phase of the meditation, which particular area—body sensations, mental imagery, or internal talk—dominated?

In this unit, you continued to note your knee-jerk reactions but also took a global look at what happens within your body and mind during these episodes. Reflecting on your experience of noticing what happens inside you during a knee-jerk reaction, please answer these questions.

1. What did you notice first during a knee-jerk reaction—body sensations (either physical or emotional), mental imagery, or internal talk?

2. How did the process of examining your body sensations, mental imagery, and internal talk during a knee-jerk reaction cause your response to intensify or diminish?

3. Recall an especially intense knee-jerk reaction. What happened physically, emotionally, and with your internal talk and mental images?

This Week's Practices

☐ *Meditative practice—10 to 20 minutes per day:*
In this unit, you used Shinzen Young's practice to put together what you've done separately over the past several weeks—focusing first on your body, through an examination of physical sensations and emotions, then on your mental images, continuing through your self-talk, and then finishing by freely floating through your interior space.

☐ *Daily-life practice—each day:*
Continue to note your knee-jerk reactions with a focus on everything happening within your interior space during these episodes: physical sensations, emotions, mental imagery, and internal talk. Keep a list of the reactions (behaviors you immediately or later regret), with notes on what was happening in your interior space.

☐ *Reflection—15 to 30 minutes at the end of the week:*
Choose one or more questions from the Meditative Practice Questions, Daily-Life Practice Questions, or Discussion Questions above, and write about your experience.

PART 2

Understanding

In part 1 of this handbook, you focused on awareness. You cultivated your concentration and attention and became aware of many aspects of your reactivity. Now, in part 2, you will see where this reactivity comes from. You will begin with the Cycle of Reactivity.

As you can see in the accompanying diagram—and may have noticed through your practice of noticing your knee-jerk reactions—the Cycle of Reactivity runs much of your life.

Here's how the Cycle begins for each of us. Through our senses, we take in **data**—raw information about the world. We see a coworker, for example: *Oh, that's Mark.* We filter our awareness through our **assumptions** about how the world is—*He should stop wasting my time*—and how we think it should be—*I wish he'd leave me alone.* The combination of awareness and assumptions leads to **feelings** of like, neutrality, or dislike. If we cling to these feelings, we convert them to the states of **craving** (*I want that, I have to have it*), **delusion** (misunderstanding of reality, often with a refusal to learn), or **aversion** (*I don't want that, keep it away from me*). In the case of seeing Mark, the state is aversion.

These states lead to knee-jerk reactions—for example, pretending we didn't see Mark and ducking into the restroom. Or we could interact with Mark with a negative mindset: we might say something that drives a further wedge into our work and personal relationships, jeopardizing projects and morale.

You'll explore the Cycle of Reactivity in your own life, and later you'll look at ways you can break the cycle.

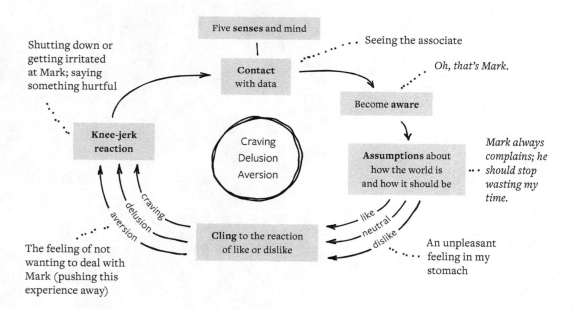

I Observe the Cycle of Reactivity in My Life

Introduction

After closely watching your knee-jerk reactions during the past several weeks, you probably will not be surprised to learn that about 90 percent of human behavior is automatic. Similar situations and circumstances will elicit the same responses; whether getting stuck in traffic or dealing with difficult people, we spend most of our lives reacting without thinking.

Automatic doesn't need to mean "bad," of course. We could not function in the world without many automatic responses; it would be hard to drive a car if we had to consider what to do in every moment. The more we can develop skillful and useful automatic behaviors, the better.

Unfortunately, if you're like most of us, far too many of your actions are negative reactions rather than appropriate responses. Knee-jerk reactions are those you immediately or later regret. They result from the Cycle of Reactivity, which begins when you encounter data—some raw information about your situation.

Perhaps you look at your calendar and see that you're scheduled to make a presentation on Friday—the **data**. Then you become **aware**: *Oh, that's tomorrow, and I still don't have it finished because logistics hasn't come through with the numbers.*

Your **awareness** is then filtered through your **assumptions**—the stories you tell yourself—about how the world is and how it should be. *Logistics never responds in a timely way; it's a wonder the supply chain hasn't fallen apart.*

Your assumptions produce **feelings** of like, neutrality, or dislike—in this scenario, dislike.

By **clinging** to reactions of like or dislike, you convert them into the states of **craving**, **delusion**, or, in this case, **aversion**. *I hate working with the logistics team.*

Any of these states will then give rise to a **knee-jerk reaction**: maybe you fire off a snippy email to logistics. Or you might withdraw and stop working on your presentation altogether.

As you can see, the Cycle offers several moments when a different response could change the result. In the next unit, for example, you'll work with your assumptions about the world—perhaps the most powerful place to break the Cycle of Reactivity. Your assumptions—the stories you believe—act as filters that take the simple neutral information the world presents to you and turns it into feelings of craving (*Oh, I read that new game is incredible, I have to buy it now—it can just go on the credit card!*) or aversion (*People from that political party are always idiots—I'm going to hate this guy*).

Start by examining the three poisons of the mind that drive the cycle: craving, aversion, and delusion.

> **Craving** is an intense desire to possess people, things, or experiences. It can show up as greed, lust, desire, avarice, or stinginess. *I want that person. I have to have that jacket. I need my money; I can't spare any for a tip.*

> **Aversion** is the intense desire to rid yourself of people, things, and situations. It often manifests as anger, fear, sadness, anxiety, disgust, irritation, or worry. *I hate people of that political persuasion. I'm scared to make my presentation to the group. What if my child gets hurt on that camping trip?*

> **Delusion** is the refusal to learn in light of new information that could upset your worldview. It might reveal itself as pride, arrogance, self-righteousness, or aloofness. *I know all I need to know about that. I'm not interested in what someone like that has to say.*

These poisons fuel the responses of like and dislike, which, do not forget, are physical as well as mental. For example, in addition to making you angry or worried, aversion can manifest in your body as a heightened heart rate or knot in your gut. *I feel sick when I see my ex. That politician is ruining this country.*

But here's the important point: liking or not liking something isn't the problem. Even the Dalai Lama experiences dislike.

*It's your **clinging** to feelings of like or dislike that fuels reactivity.*

You understand this intuitively: *Worrying about it won't help. My being angry is only making this worse.* But too often you try to *suppress* your feelings, shoving the like or dislike into the back of your mind, where it simmers; or you *amplify* your feelings, blowing up and pushing them onto someone else.

Neither response is healthy. Suppression often turns into amplification, when months or years of pent-up feelings explode.

A better alternative, which we've discussed before, is equanimity—noticing your feelings in some difficult situation but taking a step back and accepting them. With acceptance, you can then act in an appropriate way.

Mindfulness, too, can help transform your response, as can kindness, compassion, and generosity.

Exercise

Since the beginning of this program, you've been paying attention to your knee-jerk reactions, first simply noting them and then examining more and more closely just what's happening within your mind and body when you're having them.

In this exercise, you'll examine the causes of your knee-jerk reactions in light of your new understanding of the Cycle of Reactivity. Feel free to refer to your journal entries and previous reflections about knee-jerk reactions. Please use your journal to record your responses to the following questions.

1. What kinds of outer situations typically led to your knee-jerk reactions?

2. In those cases, would you say the outer situation *caused* the knee-jerk reaction? Or was it more complicated than that?

3. What patterns did you notice in your knee-jerk reactions? What patterns did you notice in the situations in which you had such reactions? What patterns did you notice in the feelings you had about those situations?

4. When you cling to feelings of like or dislike, do you feel happiness and peace or anxiety and irritation? Expand on your answer.

5. Consider one of the times you had a knee-jerk reaction. Did you experience aversion, delusion, or craving at the time? Why?

Reflection Questions

As you've seen, your inner life is complicated, intense, and in large measure run by automatic drives. Often, you're unconscious of those drives unless you deliberately set out to study them. Now you've begun to study not just what happens internally during knee-jerk reactions—my heart races, my stomach sinks, I have harsh thoughts about a person or situation—but how those sensations and internal talk build toward the knee-jerk reactions.

Reflecting upon your growing understanding of the Cycle of Reactivity, please consider and answer the following questions, recording your answers in your journal.

1. As you became more skilled in monitoring yourself during knee-jerk reactions, which sensations, feelings, mental images, or internal talk tended to reliably drop you into a Cycle of Reactivity?

2. You've learned that you interpret the data you encounter each day partly based on your assumptions about how the world is and how it should be. Which of your assumptions surprised you?

3. How has the process of monitoring your knee-jerk reactions led you to challenge or change some of your assumptions?

4. We're defining *craving* as an attachment to getting what we like and *aversion* as an attachment to avoiding what we dislike. What's wrong with wanting to have what we love or wanting to ward off things we hate? How does that cause suffering? (Remember, having likes and dislikes is normal: it's *clinging* to them that creates suffering.)

5. The third poison of the mind is delusion, the refusal to learn anything that might threaten our identities and the sense of security we draw from them. Do you agree that delusion, as we've defined it, causes suffering? Or is delusion a means of maintaining psychological safety? Explain your position.

Discussion Questions

You've learned that up to 90 percent of your life is ruled by responses you make without thought. You've learned that knee-jerk reactions are the culmination of the Cycle of Reactivity. And you've learned that at any given moment, your interior landscape is a tumble of activity as you come into contact with information about your surroundings.

Now that you've had an opportunity to reflect individually on your growing understanding of reactivity in your own life, please reflect on the experience as a group.

1. What patterns have you noticed in your knee-jerk reactions?

2. Having practiced, where do you now first recognize you are caught in the Cycle?

3. How has the process of noticing your feelings and the physical sensations that go with them helped you to observe them without becoming subject to them?

4. Do you now feel more accepting of situations beyond your control? If so, in what ways has that changed your behavior and your life?

5. Which is the strongest poison in your life—aversion, delusion, or craving? What benefits do you gain from it?

This Week's Practices

☐ *Meditative practice—10 to 20 minutes per day:*

For this unit's meditative practice, we'd like to bring your attention back to the body, that is, to both physiological sensations and emotional feelings. Shinzen Young uses the phrases "feel out" for physical sensations and "feel in" for feeling flavors. As you become aware of either one arising in your body, you can simply note it or you can label it (aloud or to yourself), using the phrases "feel in" and "feel out." Following the general guidelines for meditative practices in part 1, we suggest you set a timer for 10 to 20 minutes and note "feel in," "feel out," or "none" each day this week.

☐ *Daily-life practice—each day:*

As soon as you become aware of a knee-jerk reaction, stop and focus on your body. See whether you can detect clinging to feelings of like, dislike, or neutrality. Determine which is most prominent: craving, aversion, or delusion.

In addition, do the exercise from this chapter using your own experience and data. You can then include your responses to this exercise in your weekly reflection.

☐ *Reflection—15 to 30 minutes at the end of the week:*

Choose one or more questions from the Exercise, Reflection Questions, or Discussion Questions above, and write about your experience.

I Examine My Assumptions

Introduction

According to author and teacher Byron Katie in *Loving What Is*, "The only time we suffer is when we believe a thought that argues with what is. When the mind is perfectly clear, what is is what we want."[3]

In this unit, we introduce a practice that can help you dismantle the Cycle of Reactivity.

By learning to surface and examine your assumptions about how the world is and how it should be, you can weaken one of the strongest links in the Cycle.

"If you want reality to be different than it is, you might as well try to teach a cat to bark," Katie says. "You can try and try, and in the end the cat will look up at you and say, 'Meow.'"[4]

Katie believes that those things we believe shouldn't have happened "*should* have happened. It should have happened because it did, and no thinking in the world can change it."[5] The payoff, she says, is that when we stop arguing with reality, our lives become "simple, fluid, kind, and fearless."[6]

Please visit Byron Katie's website, www.thework.com, and download "The Work of Byron Katie," which contains a distilled version of her worksheet-based process, including examples. Download Katie's "Worksheet," too, as well as her one-page description of how to do The Work. Katie makes all this material available for free on her site.

"It should have happened because it did, and no thinking in the world can change it."

---

3 Bryon Katie, *Loving What Is: Four Questions That Can Change Your Life*, in collaboration with Stephen Mitchell (New York: Harmony Books, 2002), 1.

4 Ibid.

5 Ibid, 2.

6 Ibid.

You will use the Worksheet to help you identify your assumptions, and then you'll examine each assumption, guided by Katie's four questions:

1. Is it true?

2. Can you absolutely know it's true?

3. How do you react, what happens, when you believe that thought?

4. Who or what would you be without the thought?[7]

Then you'll turn the thought around and find specific, genuine examples of how the opposites of your assumptions might be as true or truer.

Let's say a chatty coworker stops by your desk.

THE THOUGHT: *Mike is about to waste my time!*

1. But is it true? *Yes!*

2. Can you absolutely know it's true? *No.* (Your thought process here might be as follows: *Well, he does interrupt me. But chances are I'd be getting up for a cup of coffee in the next five minutes anyway. And of course, I don't know yet what he's going to say. Maybe it won't be a waste.*)

3. How do you react when you believe that thought? *I get edgy and impatient and close my ears to whatever he's saying.*

4. Who would you be without that thought? *I'd be a happier and better coworker, and I might gain insights into my work by listening to Mike.*

For your meditative practice this week, you'll choose a challenging situation and person, and do The Work at least once. You'll need to find some quiet time to fill in the worksheet and to follow the instructions for posing the questions. This process usually takes between half an hour and an hour. We recommend that you not begin with the most challenging person and situation in your life.

When you're not doing The Work, you may find it fruitful to continue one of the previous meditative practices, whether it's noting body sensations ("feel out" and "feel in"), watching the breath, or one of the other practices from part 1.

7　Byron Katie, "Judge-Your-Neighbor Worksheet," *The Work of Byron Katie,* https://thework.com/wp-content/uploads/2019/02/jyn_en_mod_6feb2019_r4_form1.pdf.

For your daily practice, you'll use an abbreviated version of The Work whenever you notice your inner talk is using the words "should" or "shouldn't." When you hear the inner voice say, *should*, you want to ask yourself, "Is it true?" So, if you hear the inner voice say, *The boss should give me more time to complete this job*, immediately ask yourself, "Is it true?"

Likewise, when you hear the inner voice say, *shouldn't*, you will remind yourself, "But it is." So, if you hear, *There shouldn't be so much traffic*, you'll remind yourself, "But there already is."

Exercise

In this unit, you attack the Cycle of Reactivity by surfacing and examining your assumptions about how the world is and how it should be. You've already seen how your assumptions can lead to actions you later regret; but ridding yourself of them is not as simple as waving a wand. You'll need to work to examine your assumptions. You'll do so through the lens of what Byron Katie calls "The Work."

You'll use Katie's "Judge-Your-Neighbor Worksheet," available on her website. Choose a challenging situation and person—but, at this point, perhaps not the most *challenging—and take thirty to sixty minutes to fill in the "Judge-Your-Neighbor Worksheet" and to investigate your statements with the four questions and the turnarounds. Complete the exercise in writing, not just in your head—perhaps in your journal, or perhaps in some document you can then delete or destroy.*

Reflection Questions

As you completed the worksheet about someone you haven't yet forgiven and then did The Work, you began the process of dismantling the Cycle of Reactivity. Questioning your assumptions, you were afforded an opportunity to look at parts of your life—and thinking—in a new way.

Please use the following questions to record in your journal your realizations from this practice. Allow yourself to consult your worksheet and notes.

1. Describe your experience of surfacing your feelings about a person you haven't forgiven.

2. What emotions showed up for you when you thought about how you want that person to change?

3. Consider one belief about what that person should or should not do—how does that belief make you feel? How might you tend to react when gripping that belief?

4. You stated what you hoped never to experience again with that person—then you turned that statement around. How did that process feel?

5. Having gone through this exercise, how do you feel about this person now? How do you feel about yourself?

Discussion Questions

In your meditative practice of doing The Work, you've had an opportunity to examine what your life could be like if you shed yourself of assumptions about one or more people in your life. In your daily-life practice, you've questioned your inner voice's statements about the way things should or shouldn't be.

Now here are some questions that will help you explore your realizations with a group.

1. How did it make you feel to question your inner statements about the way things should or shouldn't be? How did that questioning change your expectations or behavior?

2. After going through the worksheet, challenging your assumptions, how did your feelings about a person you haven't forgiven change? Do you still want that person to change?

3. When you envisioned yourself without your assumptions about that person, what feelings came up for you?

4. When you flipped your assumptions, how did your feelings about the other person shift? How did your feelings about yourself shift?

5. When you came to the flip for question 6 in The Work, what kind of resistance did you feel to the idea of experiencing something with the person you had hoped you'd never experience again? Where did that resistance come from?

This Week's Practices

☐ *Meditative practice—10 to 20 minutes per day:*
Do The Work at least once. If you wish, revisit previous meditative practices, such as counting breaths or noting body sensations ("feel in" and "feel out").

☐ *Daily-life practice—each day:*
Listen for internal talk saying *should* or *shouldn't*. When you hear *should*, ask yourself, "Is it true?" When you hear *shouldn't*, say to yourself, "But it is."

☐ *Reflection—15 to 30 minutes at the end of the week:*
Choose one or more questions from the Reflection Questions or Discussion Questions above, and write about your experience.

I Accept What Is

Introduction

Last week you began to dismantle the Cycle of Reactivity by examining your assumptions about the way the world is and ought to be. As part of your daily-life practice last week, you listened for an internal *shouldn't* and immediately countered it with the statement, "But it is."

This week you'll build on that practice by not only acknowledging your reality—what is—but also accepting it. This is important because clinging to your assumptions of how things should be, instead of surrendering to what is, can bring suffering. Here is an equation you saw earlier:

$$\text{Suffering} = \text{pain} \times \text{resistance}$$

Pain is part of nature: we will all encounter it from time to time. But the suffering usually associated with pain is optional. What this equation says is that if you can eliminate your resistance, your suffering will disappear.

It can be easy to see how resistance causes suffering in children, for example. A five-year-old who knows she's going to the doctor to get a shot might spend hours in near-hysterical fear of a small amount of pain that will likely last a second or two. As adults, we can see how much suffering she is causing herself by all that resistance—so much more suffering than the shot alone will cause.

Suffering works the same way for adults. Imagine leaving for work an hour early to avoid traffic. Shortly after you've entered the freeway, the traffic crawls to a stop. *But this can't be*, you say to yourself. *Rush hour hasn't started yet.* Your pulse quickens, and you bang the steering wheel as anxiety takes hold. But no matter how much you bang the wheel, you are still stuck in traffic. You are causing yourself suffering by resisting the reality of what is, simply because things aren't as you want them to be.

What if you gave up your assumption—that because you left early, there shouldn't be so much traffic—and accepted the reality before you? *The traffic is stuck, and I cannot move until I can move.* Now you are not causing yourself suffering because you are not resisting your reality. Can you accept each moment as if you had chosen it?

Meditative Practice

For your meditative practice this week, you will attempt to Be Here Now, a practice meant to give you an experience of what spiritual teacher Eckhart Tolle writes about in *The Power of Now*[8] and *Stillness Speaks*.[9]

Time and again, Tolle invites readers into the Now, encouraging us to become friendly with the moment at hand. Immersing ourselves in the present moment is like the feeling of coming home, where home is the place that brings us the most comfort. If we cannot feel at home in the present moment then no matter where we go, we will always feel discomfort within us.

Tolle also challenges our sense of what Now is, and in so doing enlarges our sense of who we are. Now is not what occurs in the present moment though that is what most of us believe. It is instead the context within which everything occurs.

Another recurring Tolle theme, closely aligned with being in the Now, is acceptance of what is—of saying "yes" to what is. We often think of acceptance in terms of embracing the bad—*I have the flu and my body hurts*—without judgment. Tolle acknowledges that is part of what acceptance means, noting that when we accept the things that seem least acceptable in this world, we have sourced our greatest access to grace.

But he enlarges the meaning of acceptance, too, acknowledging that as human beings, we often have difficulty accepting our Now. A parent who misses a flight and can't get to a child's graduation, for example, might understandably have trouble accepting such an event. *This isn't fair! This shouldn't have happened to me.* But Tolle notes that the things we can fully accept offer us a pathway to peace, particularly acceptance of the resistance we feel to accepting what we have deemed unacceptable.

But—crucially—Tolle notes that while it is essential we accept what is *internally*, we don't necessarily have to accept the external state of affairs. Let's say you purchase the latest smartphone from your cell phone carrier, and when it arrives it doesn't function properly. You might think Tolle is telling you to accept the broken phone as it is. What Tolle is in fact encouraging you to do is to accept the state of your cell phone without internal or external emotional complaint: its brokenness is real.

---

8 Eckhart Tolle, *The Power of Now: A Guide to Spiritual Enlightenment* (Novato, CA: New World Library, 1999).

9 Tolle, *Stillness Speaks* (Vancouver: Namaste Publishing, 2003).

What you do next is important. If you call your cellular provider, let them know the phone is broken, and ask for their assistance in fixing or replacing it, you are not complaining. You are addressing your circumstances.

If, however, you berate the employee on the other end of the line and shout at them for having sent you a broken phone, you are likely to create a defensive or reactive posture in them. You might elicit a response like, "I've never heard of our sending someone a broken phone. Maybe you're the one who broke it!"

If you do call and yell at the employee but they are present to the moment, they will hear and experience your ego but not define you by how it is showing up. Recognizing the human being under the ego, they will work with you to repair or replace the defective phone.

The meditative practice for this unit is to Be Here Now. That sounds simple. But when your mind wanders and you're not aware of what's happening both within and without, you're not really here and you're not in the Now.

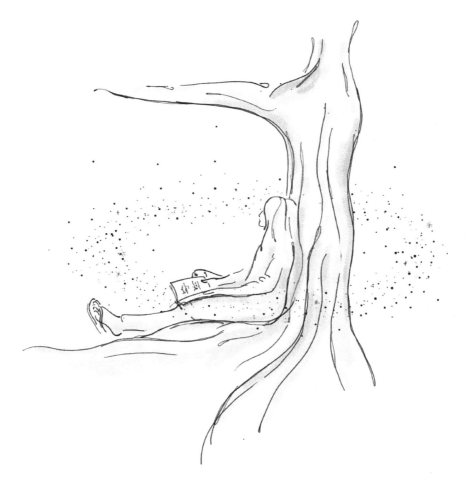

As with all the meditations in this handbook, we suggest you play a recording of the meditation so you can focus on the practice instead of trying to read and meditate simultaneously. You can use a version of this meditation that we have prerecorded and made available at www.psm-handbook.com, or you can record yourself reading the meditation aloud.

Find a position that allows you to stay sharp—alert yet reposed. For most people, this will involve sitting. But if you're feeling sleepy or fuzzy, it's okay to stand in place.

Be here Now.

This moment may seem like just one moment among many others stretching out from the past into the future. And yet, this moment is Now, right Now.

This, right Here, is the present moment.

This present moment is always Here. No matter where you go, no matter what you do, it is always Now.

Settle into this moment. Allow your breath to settle.

Notice that when you breathe in, it is Now. And as you breathe out, it is Now.

Let yourself become aware of the full sensation of your breath in this moment.

Expand your awareness and notice that your thoughts are happening Now, too.

Watch your thoughts. They come and go. Notice how you may want to go with them to somewhere other than Here and some time other than Now. Memories of past interactions and worries about future ones crowd in. There are things you need to remember to do. You are distracted by sounds and sensations and end up being lost in one thought after another.

Notice that when you follow these thoughts, you're no longer Here—you lose contact with Now.

Simply come back to the present moment.

Be Here. Now.

See if you can stay Here for a while.

Spend a little time exploring this moment.

What is the quality of Now? What does it sound like?

How does Now feel?

How deep is Now? How long is Now?

Can Now hold more and more of your experience?

Notice what is happening around you. You may be aware, either directly or indirectly, of all sorts of things.

Are you resisting anything that is happening right Now? Is something happening that you really like? Maybe there is something you're indifferent to.

Notice how many opinions you have about the experience of this moment.

Go a little deeper.

Do you want to be Here right Now? Do you want this—whatever this is—to be happening right Now?

Do you think it should be different? More of this and less of that?

Notice all these judgments.

Notice that this moment is really happening.

Verify this for yourself: despite all your opinions, stories, likes, and dislikes, this present moment is just as it is.

Then try this experiment: what if you fully accepted this moment exactly as it is? This moment. Don't try to change anything about it; just experience it fully. Experience it Now.

This moment is true. It is what it is, or more simply, it is. Now.

What is happening . . . is. Perhaps change will come, but this moment is. This moment right Now. Perhaps you will help change what happens next, but this moment is happening Now.

See how much of this moment you can fully accept. And this moment, Now.

Practice accepting what is.

Is there an uncomfortable sensation in your body? It could be anything from a mild discomfort to something more painful.

See if you can experience it just as it is.

Don't push it away. Don't make it more than it is. Don't create a story about it.

Just be with it.

Maybe even explore it. What does it feel like? Does it have texture, color, a smell, a sound, or other attributes?

Practice accepting it as it is.

Scan your whole being.

Do you notice any tense spots, any places you're pushing away? Anything you're holding onto?

For each of these places, practice saying "yes" to the full experience. Accept it just the way it is Now.

See how much of the experience of this present moment you can accept—letting it be as it is.

When you're ready, bring your awareness to the day ahead. How will you experience this day?

How much of this day can you experience from your own present Now?

This is an invitation, an invitation into the ever-present Now.

Daily-Life Practice

For your daily-life practice, you'll focus on saying "yes" to what is. Surrendering to and accepting reality may seem passive, but the acceptance we mean is something different. It is your unconditional acceptance of what is, in fact, already the case, an internal alignment with the way things are. There is no need to argue with or deny its existence. Instead, surrender to the existence of the objective state of affairs, and accept your subjective reactions to it. Then, if action is called for, you can respond appropriately.

The practice of saying "yes" to what is directly addresses the equation **suffering = pain × resistance**. When you resist reality, you cause yourself to suffer. By clinging to assumptions about how things should be rather than accepting how they are, you launch yourself into the Cycle of Reactivity. By accepting each moment as if you had chosen it, you reduce reactivity and cultivate presence.

For example:

1. *I've just received a potentially serious diagnosis. I accept that reality.*

2. *I am angry and afraid. I don't want to be sick. I accept those feelings.*

3. *Accepting those two realities, I will now proceed to work with my doctors to find a way to address this diagnosis. As each new fact presents itself in the process, and as each new feeling about those facts arises, I accept them all. I don't increase my suffering by resisting either the facts or my feelings.*

A key to acceptance is either to be free of assumptions about how things should be—unlikely for most of us humans—or to be willing to let go of those assumptions when confronted with a reality that clashes with them.

As you do the daily-life practice of saying "yes" to what is, please record your experiences for the week. Note when your expectations about how things should be weren't met, and then practice releasing them as in the example below:

When I entered the break room, **I expected** the coffee pot to be full.

But it wasn't.

I say "yes" to the empty pot and to the reality that I must make a new pot if I want coffee.

In your journal, use the following template, and record as many examples as you can.

1. When _____, I expected _____.

2. But _____, and I say "yes" to _____.

Reflection Questions

In this unit, you placed your focus on acceptance, on surrendering to what is. In doing so, you also honed your ability to be present.

As part of your meditative and daily-life practices, you tried to accept those things in your life that did not bear out your expectations while also accepting your subjective reactions to them. The Dalai Lama does not like China's policy toward Tibet, but he does not get stuck in his anger and aversion toward the policy, which, after all, will not change it. At the same time, he does not deny his anger and aversion, stuff it down deep inside himself. He acknowledges both the reality of a policy he dislikes and his feelings about it. Consequently, he is in alignment with reality.

Please use the following questions to reflect upon your experience with these practices.

1. Eckhart Tolle invites you to recognize that the present moment simply is. He asks if you can allow it to be what it is, without the need to change it. What does this mean to you, and how can you use it in your daily life?

2. According to Tolle, acceptance of what is does not mean one ought not try to change a situation. How can you both accept a situation and look to change it? Did such an opportunity arise for you this week?

3. What was the hardest thing you had to accept this week? What was the easiest?

4. Recall a time in the past week when the best you could do was accept the fact that you had difficulty accepting what is. Describe what happened and your reaction. Then explain how you feel about the situation now.

5. Earlier in this handbook, you were likely surprised to learn how much of your life is ruled without thought, including knee-jerk reactions. What surprised you this week as you saw how often you had to consciously accept things that did not square with your assumptions?

Discussion Questions

According to Tolle, when you can accept the things that are least acceptable in this world, you have sourced your greatest access to grace. And yet acceptance can be one of the most difficult things a person can do. In this unit, you worked on surrendering to what is—even if your acceptance was limited to accepting the fact that you could not surrender to what is.

Now please discuss your experience with this practice as a group, using the following questions as a starting point.

1. This week, you revisited the equation, suffering = pain × resistance. How have you seen this operate in your own life? Did you notice a difference in how it operated this week as you practiced acceptance?

2. Your practice this week took direct aim at your assumptions. Although you just started, how do you feel changed by this work?

3. Tolle promises that when your attention moves into the Now, you experience an awakening as if you've come out of a dream state. What did it feel like to experience that feeling of being awake this week?

4. You were challenged this week to say "yes" to what is, defined as accepting each moment as though you had chosen it. What difficulties did you have with this practice? What breakthroughs did you have with this practice?

5. We shared the example of receiving a broken phone and calling your cellular provider to address the situation. In what ways were you the customer this week? How were you the customer service representative?

This Week's Practices

☐ *Meditative practice—10 to 20 minutes per day:*
Be Here Now.

☐ *Daily-life practice—each day:*
Say "yes" to what is.

☐ *Reflection—15 to 30 minutes at the end of the week:*
Choose one or more questions from the Reflection Questions and Discussion Questions above, and write about your experience.

I Am in Control of My Response

Introduction

Last week, you attacked the Cycle of Reactivity by focusing on accepting your situations as they are, by saying "yes" to your Now as though you'd chosen it for yourself. This week, you will shift your focus to nurturing your ability to be responsible in the face of whatever life presents.

Think about how often you play the victim in your life. How many times have you said something like, "I'm sorry I was late to the meeting, but traffic was terrible," or "The photocopier broke so I don't have handouts to give you."

Writer and teacher Fred Kofman says these moments come up for you because you make a deal with the devil, trading power for innocence. The traffic and photocopier are outside your control, making you an apparently innocent victim.

But Kofman argues that you're abdicating responsibility when you allow yourself to rest on such excuses. Instead, you could be responsible to what life presents you. In other words, you can always be "response-able," free to choose your response to what life presents. Rather than being a "victim," Kofman says you could be a "player" in your own life. That way, things don't happen to you. Things happen, and you respond to them as challenges.[10]

Novelist and essayist David Foster Wallace mines a similar vein in his Kenyon College commencement address:[11] you have the power to choose how to interpret the things that happen all around you.

---

10 Fred Kofman, "Be a Player, Not a Victim – LinkedIn Speaker Series," YouTube video, 12:56, August 12, 2013, https://www.youtube.com/watch?v=xXdN5kMioRQ.

11 David Foster Wallace, "This Is Water," YouTube, 22:43, from a commencement speech to Kenyon College class of 2005, posted by Jamie Sullivan, May 19, 2013, https://www.youtube.com/watch?v=8CrOL-ydFMI.

Exercise

Please watch Fred Kofman's video "Be a Player, Not a Victim" and listen to David Foster Wallace's Kenyon College commencement speech "This is Water," both of which are available online.

Wallace stresses that the assumptions you hold about the world and how it should work are simply your natural default. He argues that you have the power to choose to alter your assumptions and so view the world in a different light.

Please record in your journal your responses to the following questions.

1. What do you think of Kofman's notion of response-ability? Does it ring true? Why or why not?

2. Kofman argues that even in the most extreme circumstances (for example, Viktor Frankl in the concentration camp), we can be responsible to what life presents. Do you agree, or are there times you see a limit to response-ability?

3. Where have you noticed occasions when you slipped into a victim's stance? Were you able to shift to the stance of a player? If so, how?

4. Wallace says that his experience of life supports his perspective that the universe revolves around him. Think about your last interaction with another person and imagine what it was like from their point of view. How do you think you showed up for the other person?

5. According to Wallace, learning how to think is about choosing where to place your attention and choosing how to make meaning from life's experiences. In what ways does this idea give you a sense of empowerment? How can you use it in your own life?

6. Wallace suggests that it is during times of irritation when the opportunity to choose where you place your attention is most alive. Since listening to his speech, how did it go when you chose to view a frustrating situation through a different lens?

7. Wallace notes that throwing off your assumptions is difficult, requiring intention and practice, and that some days you won't be up to the task or won't even have the energy to try. What does it cost you to remain committed to, and entrenched in, your assumptions?

8. Wallace acknowledges that there's an allure to the freedom to be the ruler of the world you create in your mind. But he offers that the most precious kind of freedom is the freedom to remain aware of where you place your attention and to live in service of others in the small ways that go uncelebrated day after day. What are the advantages and disadvantages of both of these types of freedom?

Reflection Questions

Fred Kofman says you can be responsible to what life presents you. David Foster Wallace believes you have the power to choose how you interpret the events in your unfolding life and how you respond.

To help you reflect on this unit's messages and your efforts to incorporate them in your life, please answer in your journal the following questions.

1. What was your initial emotional response to Kofman's assertion about unconditional response-ability? Did it sound liberating? Oppressive? Did you feel empowered? Fearful? Angry? Why?

2. Kofman makes a distinction between being "responsible to" what life presents versus being "responsible for" what you encounter. How often in the past week have you rebelled against being responsible for something before realizing that you had to be responsible to it?

3. How can being responsible to what life presents help you break the Cycle of Reactivity?

4. What challenges did you face this week? How did you respond to those challenges—automatically or consciously? In what ways were you a victim? In what ways were you a player?

5. Wallace, noting that we all worship something, says there's no such thing as atheism. What do you worship, and how does it shape your response to what life presents you?

6. Did you notice instances in which you caught yourself thinking an automatic thought about a person or situation? Which thoughts did you continue? Under which circumstances did you drop your assumptions and reconsider the person or situation?

Discussion Questions

As you learn how to remain aware and to focus your attention by your own choosing, you find there are alternatives to your irritation with life's inconvenient moments. You have the ability to experience the beauty of your own boredom or to laugh at your frustration when communicating with your internet provider. David Foster Wallace speaks of the sacredness of these opportunities, placing them on par with the mysteries of our creation and of the universe itself.

These abilities, arising from awareness and choice, come from accepting the Now as though you had chosen it for yourself. In order to develop them, you have to make a conscious choice to be responsible to life as it is.

You've had an opportunity to reflect on these principles alone. Here are some questions you can use as a starting point for discussions with others.

1. Fred Kofman asks whether you want to be a victim or a player. In what ways were you a victim this week? In what ways were you a player? Did one serve you better than the other?

2. According to Kofman, being a player gives you freedom. That freedom is, however, conditional: "Freedom does not mean doing what you want without consequences; it means having the capacity to choose, in the face of a situation, the response that is most consistent with your values."[12] What changes do you have to make to gain the freedom of acting in accordance with your values?

3. Think about a moment in which you felt frustration during the past week. What role did your assumptions play in that frustration? Were you able to drop those assumptions? If so, how did that affect your feeling of frustration?

4. In his speech, Wallace relates the story of standing in a long line at a crowded grocery store after a trying day at work. He notes that unless he makes a conscious decision about how to think and what to pay attention to, he's going to find himself deeply unhappy each time he enters a store. Did you try this week to think and focus differently? Whether you did or didn't, what was the result?

5. According to Wallace, we move through life with the attitude that the world revolves around us. How did this land with you? Were you able to see any life events through the eyes of others?

---

12 Fred Kofman, *Conscious Business: How to Build Value through Values* (Louisville, CO: Sounds True, 2013), 43.

This Week's Practices

☐ *Meditative practice—10 to 20 minutes per day:*
As you deepen your understanding of how the Cycle of Reactivity operates in your own life—and as you hone your ability to dismantle it—you need to build your concentration, clarity, and equanimity with respect to what goes on in your body and mind. This week we suggest repeating the meditative practice from part 1, unit 4.

☐ *Daily-life practice—each day:*
Be sensitive this week to the times you find yourself in a victim's stance. What are the circumstances? Are there patterns? Assuming you are able to shift to the stance of the player, how do you do so?

☐ *Reflection—15 to 30 minutes at the end of the week:*
Choose one or more questions from the Exercise, Reflection Questions, or Discussion Questions above, and write about your experience.

PART 3

Transformation

You have come to the third and final part of this handbook.

We called part 1 "Awareness" because the practices it contains help us to see just how reactive we generally are and to observe the thoughts, feelings, and sensations associated with our reactivity.

Part 2 focused on "Understanding": by introducing the Cycle of Reactivity along with the works of Byron Katie, Eckhart Tolle, Fred Kofman, and David Foster Wallace, we sought to deepen your understanding of where your reactivity comes from and to explore ways of undoing it.

In this part, we introduce practices that transform automatic reactivity into appropriate response. We offer several meditative and daily-life practices. And we introduce three response practices, all focused on developing your ability to engage in skillful speech.

I Experience Life Fully

Introduction

In this unit, you'll work to develop a broader, more complete view of self through Ken McLeod's Opening Practice, which will be your meditative practice for the week.

In addition, you'll explore what we call the Gateways to Presence, daily-life practices that bring you into the present so that you can experience life more fully. In subsequent units, you'll build on your knowledge of the Gateways to Presence and incorporate more of these practices into your life.

Meditative Practice

As always, we suggest you play a recording of the meditation so you can focus on the practice instead of trying to read and meditate simultaneously. You can use a version of this meditation that we have prerecorded and made available at www.psm-handbook.com, or you can record yourself reading the meditation aloud.

Please find a quiet place where you can be uninterrupted for about fifteen or twenty minutes. If you need to find such a place, wait until you find it before continuing.

Adopt a position that allows you to be alert and relaxed. Make sure to sit up straight, whether you choose to sit on the floor or in a chair. If you become sleepy or dull during this practice, try straightening your spine or standing up. If you find you're getting tense, try taking a deep breath and relaxing your shoulders on the out-breath.

Keeping your eyes open, rest in the **experience of breathing**. Rather than think of yourself—"me"—watching the breath, open yourself to the experience of breathing. This involves opening yourself to the experience of your body as it does the breathing.

Feel all the **parts of the body** that are engaged in breathing—nose, lungs, abdomen, heart, mouth. Now notice the tactile sensations of the breath moving through the nostrils, the back of your throat, into your lungs, and the movement of your diaphragm as the breath moves in and out.

Now, notice all the different **emotional reactions** going on within you. Perhaps you're agitated, or you feel peace or a sense of relief.

Next, pay attention to the **thoughts and stories** that come and go.

All of these are part of the experience of breathing. In addition, your experience of breathing right now includes everything you experience through your senses—the shadow that darkens the room when clouds pass the sun, the sound of car motors, and the physical sensations of your body resting on a chair or your clothes in contact with your skin.

Can you **experience all of this simultaneously**, not moving attention around from one part to another, but opening to experience everything at the same time? If you find this challenging, that's okay. Just be, and allow yourself to experience the Now.

Let your heart open to everything you experience. Let go of judging what you experience, whether as good or bad. You might feel like there's a kind of softening inside. Perhaps you feel fear or discomfort. Experience all of that, free of judgment, along with everything else.

Now, ask yourself this question: **"Who or what experiences all of this?"** There is no need to answer. Simply rest in the shift you may experience when you ask the question. "Who or what experiences all of this?"

If you do experience a shift, let go of the need to hold onto it. Return to experiencing everything that arises in awareness. Include it all. Then ask again, "Who or what experiences all this?"

This practice is a way of opening to your life. As you do this, **notice what happens to your sense of yourself—your sense of "me."**

Meditative Practice Questions

For your meditative practice this week, you experienced Ken McLeod's Opening Practice as a way of opening yourself to your life.

To help you reflect on your meditation, please consider and answer the following questions.

1. During the first part of the meditation, you ran a checklist and focused on various aspects of your breathing, your body, and your thoughts and emotions. Later, you tried to experience all that was happening at the same time. To what degree were you able to experience everything at the same time, and what did you experience?

2. What did you feel, both emotionally and physically, when you opened your heart to everything you experienced? Did you feel these things with or without judgment?

3. Toward the end of the meditation, you were directed to ask—but not answer— "Who or what experiences all of this?" In what ways did your consciousness shift when you asked that question? What is your sense of who or what experienced all those things?

4. McLeod's meditation concludes by asking what this way of opening to your life does to your sense of yourself. Did you conclude with a larger or smaller sense of self? In what ways?

Daily-Life Practice

A client meeting runs longer than expected. You feel your stomach knot and fists clench; you're going to be late for your next appointment. You feel frustration welling up in you and resentment toward the client for taking the first ten minutes of the meeting recounting his exploits on the golf course.

But as he walks across the room to gather his buy orders, you watch your breathing. You feel the cool air come in through your nostrils and fill your lungs, and the warm air rush out. Two more watched breaths and the client returns with the orders. Your stomach is unknotted, and your frustration and resentment have ebbed.

Although you're still going to be late to your next appointment, you've brought yourself into the present moment using some of the Gateways to Presence: you watched your breath and noted body sensations. From this place, you found your way to a third gateway: saying "yes" to what is, accepting the moment as if you had chosen it.

Through your work in this program, you've developed tools that bring you into the present moment, the Now. You've also become more attuned to what leads you into the Cycle of Reactivity and ultimately to knee-jerk reactions.

Over the years, we have gathered a number of practices that can help you to end the Cycle of Reactivity, to get you out of your mind and into what is actually happening right now. We call them the Gateways to Presence. You'll find the full list below. Several practices will be familiar from your work so far. We will introduce others in the remaining units.

Gateways to Presence

1. Observe your breathing.

2. Note body sensations ("touch" or "feel," quality, location, intensity).

3. Pay attention to "gentle touches," such as the feel of a pen in your hand.

4. Listen to the silence.

5. Bring greater attention to sense perceptions (by looking and listening without labeling).

6. Do one thing at a time.

7. Treat this moment as an end in itself, not as a means to some other end.

8. Say "yes" to what is. (Accept this moment as if you had chosen it.)

9. Practice "metta" in daily life.

10. Practice "tonglen" in daily life.

11. Engage in skillful speech.

12. Cultivate generosity (participate in the flow of giving and receiving).

13. Celebrate the success of others.

14. Pause and take one, two, or three conscious breaths.

15. Be mindful of transitions.

The daily-life practice for this unit is to use one or more of the Gateways to Presence whenever you feel yourself triggered toward reactivity. Maybe it's a traffic hassle, a disagreement with a colleague, or a lost client. Perhaps you discover that the brochures you ordered for a big presentation on Tuesday won't be ready until Thursday. *But I need these Tuesday! I'm going to call them up and chew them out.*

Once you realize you're in the Cycle of Reactivity, pull back. *Wow, my pulse is racing and my stomach feels like it's on fire.* Okay: "Do one thing at a time." And "Say 'yes' to what is." *I have the proofs. We'll make our own copies. They won't be as sharp, but we'll be able to hand them out.*

Take notes on your experiences. What happens when you drop the story and turn to one of the Gateways?

Daily-Life Practice Questions

For your daily-life practice, you used one or more of the Gateways to Presence whenever you felt triggered. Now let's see how this practice worked for you as you consider and answer the following questions.

1. Which of the Gateways to Presence were you most inclined to try as you found yourself falling into reactivity?

2. Which of the Gateways to Presence were most effective for you in stopping the Cycle of Reactivity? Which were not helpful in stopping the Cycle?

3. In which instances did you have difficulty letting go of the emotions or the assumptions that were driving you even when you tried a Gateway to Presence? What did you do, and what happened?

4. One of the Gateways to Presence is: Treat this moment as an end in itself, not as a means to some other end. What does this mean to you?

5. The Gateways to Presence are all practices that help you come into and accept what is, to be in the Now. How does being present help or hinder you once you find yourself within the Cycle of Reactivity?

Discussion Questions

For your meditative practice, you adopted Ken McLeod's Opening Practice. And for your daily-life practice, you tried some of the practices called Gateways to Presence when you felt yourself triggered toward reactivity.

You've had an opportunity to reflect on your experiences with these practices individually, and now we invite you to participate in a group discussion with the following questions as your starting point.

1. As part of the Opening Practice, you were invited to "rest in the experience of breathing." What did that feel like to you? What did you notice happening inside you?

2. Your meditative practice this week asked you to open your heart to everything you experienced as you meditated, free of judgment. In what ways did you find it difficult to let go of judgment and to open your heart?

3. In what ways did your sense of self change following your experience with the Opening Practice? Did you feel like you were a different size? A different shape? Describe the change.

4. Did you find a particular Gateway to Presence practice to be more difficult when you were reactive? For example, in what ways was it harder to do one thing at a time when you were feeling overwhelmed with anxiety?

5. As part of your daily practice, which particular Gateway to Presence did you find yourself favoring? Why do you think you found it helpful?

This Week's Practices

☐ *Meditative practice—10 to 20 minutes per day:*
Ken McLeod's Opening Practice.

☐ *Daily-life practice—each day:*
When you find yourself entering or already caught in the Cycle of Reactivity, deploy one or more of the Gateways to Presence. Note which work best for you.

☐ *Reflection—15 to 30 minutes at the end of the week:*
Choose one or more questions from the Meditative Practice Questions, Daily-Life Practice Questions, or Discussion Questions above, and write about your experience.

I Extend Kindness

Introduction

As you're driving home from work, a car cuts in front of you and nearly clips your fender. Instead of blasting your horn or shouting at the driver, you say, "May you be free from danger."

A colleague drops by your office to let you know a report she'd promised you by the end of the day now won't be ready for two days. Instead of crabbing at her or throwing your pen on the desk, you say to yourself silently, "May you live with ease."

No, you haven't gone soft or had a personality transplant. You're still a living, breathing human being with the same feelings and apprehensions we all have. You're practicing what is called *metta*, an important Gateway to Presence and one way to dissolve the apparent barriers between yourself and others.

Through your work so far, you've seen that the Cycle of Reactivity is fueled by what we've called the three poisons of the mind: craving, delusion, and aversion. Aversion comes when you cling to feelings of dislike or fear. When you're in the grip of aversion, you push away from people, holding them at arm's length. One antidote to this poison is kindness, a generalized friendliness toward others.

This week you'll do a guided metta meditation in which you'll extend kindness to six categories of people, one at a time: yourself, a benefactor, a loved one, a neutral person, someone you find difficult or with whom you are in conflict, and all beings without exception. You'll do this by wishing them safety, happiness, health, and ease.

> *The purpose of practicing metta is to foster kindness.*

For your daily-life practice, you'll engage in metta on the spot. Whether you're working with someone you like and admire or someone you see as difficult, you can extend kindness throughout your daily life by repeating your desire that the people you encounter be safe, happy, healthy, and enjoy lives of ease.

In addition, in this and the final two units, we introduce a third practice, one we call a response practice. Each of the three offers a way of responding to a person experiencing something difficult. Often, you are overwhelmed when you encounter the negative emotions of another, which can cause you to withdraw or to launch yourself into the Cycle of Reactivity. These practices help you to respond rather than react. Each contributes to your ability to engage in skillful speech, one of the Gateways to Presence.

So often, people come to you in pain or disquiet about something that's happening in their life. Your impulse is to try to fix the problem, offer advice, or suggest corrections. Parker Palmer, an educator, activist, and author, has developed an alternative approach, a method of questioning intended to "hear the other person into speech," to help them access their inner teacher.

Meditative Practice

This week, you'll engage in metta meditation, a practice that fosters kindness. You'll extend kindness to yourself, to a benefactor, to a loved one, to a neutral person, to a person you find difficult, and to all beings without exception.

Some may initially find this practice artificial and superficial. Others may wonder whether it "works." Can expressing your desire for another's happiness make that person happy? While this line of questioning is understandable, it misses a larger point: whether or not the practice helps those to whom you extend kindness, the act of extending the kindness can be helpful to *you* by growing your understanding that you are not separate from others. In fact, metta has proved to be one of the most popular and useful practices introduced in the Practice of Self-Management curriculum.

As always, we suggest you play a recording of the meditation so you can focus on the practice instead of trying to read and meditate simultaneously. You can use a version of this meditation that we have prerecorded and made available at www.psm-handbook.com, or you can record yourself reading the meditation aloud.

As usual for your meditative practice, please find a quiet place where you can be free from interruption or distraction for about fifteen or twenty minutes.

To begin, take a deep breath, feeling the cool air coming in through your nostrils and the warm air rushing out through your mouth. Take another deep breath, this time closing your eyes on the out-breath.

Breathing normally, allow your body to settle.

Begin by sending metta to yourself by repeating the following phrases, either aloud or to yourself, pausing after each phrase:

May I be free from danger. [pause]

May I be happy. [pause]

May I be healthy. [pause]

May I live with ease. [pause]

If these phrases don't touch your heart today, feel free to come up with your own language that captures the spirit of these statements. We want the practice to be meaningful to you. Perhaps you could say, "May I be free from confusion," for example, or "May I find relief from suffering." If the traditional phrases speak to your heart, that's fine. If not, use your own words to express similar wishes.

Next, move on to direct kindness toward someone you find inspiring or to whom you feel grateful. By tradition, you will call this person "the benefactor." Holding the benefactor's presence in your mind, extend to them the metta phrases:

May you be free from danger. [pause]

May you be happy. [pause]

May you be healthy. [pause]

May you live with ease. [pause]

Again, if these phrases aren't pitch-perfect to you, use your own. Perhaps your benefactor is burdened with worry or recently injured. You could say, "May you be free from your worries," or "May you recover rapidly." Again, the point is not to use the "correct" words but to use words that are meaningful to you.

Now, move on to extend kindness to a loved one or friend. Holding this person's presence in your mind, extend the metta phrases to him or to her:

May you be free from danger. [pause]

May you be happy. [pause]

May you be healthy. [pause]

May you live with ease. [pause]

As always, feel free to adjust the lines as you feel appropriate.

Next, expand metta by directing it toward those who don't usually arouse feelings of love. By moving beyond your familiar circle of loved ones, you strengthen and increase your capacity for good will.

Think of a person you neither like nor dislike. This is challenging for some people because they find it difficult to call to mind anyone they haven't labeled likable or unlikable. If this is the case for you, think about the barista who handed you your cup of coffee this morning, the grocery store clerk who checked you out during your last visit, or even a person who walks their dog past your house in the morning.

Holding this person's presence in your mind, extend the metta phrases to him or to her, remembering that it's okay to adjust them:

May you be free from danger. [pause]

May you be happy. [pause]

May you be healthy. [pause]

May you live with ease. [pause]

Now, send metta to someone with whom you've had difficulty or conflict. To do this does not mean to forget about your own needs, and it doesn't mean you must deny your own pain, anger, or fear. Extending metta to someone you consider difficult or dangerous helps you to discover and cultivate your inherent capacity for unconditional love. Still, it can be difficult to extend kindness to people you find difficult. If this is the case for you, you might consider including yourself along with the difficult person. If you want to try this, just say, "May *we* be free from danger," etc.

With this person's presence in your mind, extend the metta phrases to him or to her, again recalling that it's fine for you to adjust them if appropriate:

May you be free from danger. [pause]

May you be happy. [pause]

May you be healthy. [pause]

May you live with ease. [pause]

Finally, extend metta to all beings without exception—all people and all animals, whether you consider them pleasant or not.

Holding all beings in your mind, extend the metta phrases to them, remembering it's okay to adjust the words if appropriate:

May all beings be free from danger. [pause]

May all beings be happy. [pause]

May all beings be healthy. [pause]

May all beings live with ease. [pause]

Now, bring your attention back to your breath. Feel the cool air coming in through your nose and the warmth of the breath on your exhale. Take another deep breath and open your eyes.

Daily-Life Practice

You've just bought a new home close to the office when your supervisor asks you to come see him. He explains that the company is going through a reorganization and that your job, fortunately, has been salvaged. But you'll have to move to another state to keep it. Amid a swirl of emotions, you look at your supervisor and say to yourself:

May you be free from danger.

May you be happy.

May you be healthy.

May you live with ease.

During an important presentation, the company president is effusive in her praise of a proposal you wrote. A colleague who had little to do with the presentation, let alone the praised proposal, responds in a way that suggests he came up with the idea. You feel your face flush and heart rate increase. But instead of shooting your coworker a dirty look or interrupting to set the record straight, you feel yourself soften as you look at your coworker and say to yourself: *May you be free from danger. May you be happy. May you be healthy. May you live with ease.*

Metta was developed as a meditative practice, but it's possible to practice it in daily life. Whether you're working with someone you admire or someone you find difficult, you can repeat the four phrases to yourself.

We also recommend that you not limit the practice to those with whom you work. Metta can be especially powerful when you apply it to those you don't know, whether it's the pedestrian at the crosswalk, the barista at a coffee shop, or the dog with its head hanging out the window of a passing car.

By practicing metta in your daily life and extending kindness to all beings, you will come to see that others have the same basic desires you have: to be safe, to be happy, to be healthy, and to live with ease. This realization helps to dissolve the apparent barriers between yourself and others.

As you go through your week, practice metta on the spot with those you encounter throughout the day.

Meditative Practice and Daily-Life Practice Questions

This week, metta provided both your meditative practice and your daily-life practice. You extended kindness to yourself, to benefactors, to loved ones, to strangers, to difficult people, and to all beings.

Please consider and answer the following questions about your experience with metta, both in the context of your meditative practice and in the context of your daily-life practice.

1. In what ways, if any, did extending metta to others change your feelings about yourself and them?

2. What happened inside you when you extended kindness to yourself? To those you admire? To strangers?

3. When you practiced metta and extended kindness to difficult people in your life, what obstacles in yourself did you have to overcome?

4. What happened inside of you when you extended kindness to difficult people?

5. What did it feel like to extend kindness to all beings? What shifts do you see in the way you're viewing the world?

Response Practice

You're headed from a meeting in the conference room to your office, where you're expecting an important client call in ten minutes. As you walk down the hallway, you see a coworker. You smile and say, "How are you today?"

"Fine," your coworker says.

"Glad to hear it," you respond as you hustle toward your office. But after you take another step, you stop. Your coworker said he was fine, but the words didn't match his tone of voice. You double back. "Hey, I'm sensing that something is up. I've got a call in a few minutes. Can I check in with you later this afternoon?"

As you know from your exposure to the Gateways to Presence, one of the ways of cultivating presence is to engage in skillful speech. But it's impossible to speak skillfully if you don't listen—and real listening can prove difficult for most of us.

In a 1935 essay published in *Esquire*, Ernest Hemingway wrote, "When people talk listen completely. Don't be thinking what you're going to say. Most people never listen."[13]

It's only by truly listening that you can offer others the help they seek from you.

---

13 Ernest Hemingway, "Monologue to the Maestro: A High Seas Letter," in *By-Line Ernest Hemingway: Selected Articles and Dispatches of Four Decades*, ed. William White (New York: Charles Scribner's Sons, 1967), 219.

Parker Palmer, a writer and speaker who addresses issues ranging from education to social change, would no doubt agree.

According to Palmer, it's only by truly listening that you can offer others the help they seek from you. He has developed a set of seven guidelines for asking open and honest questions to help others access their inner teacher—and these questions can be asked successfully only if you truly listen.

Palmer has one iron-clad rule: when asking open and honest questions, there's no fixing, saving, advising, or correcting the other person.

Usually when people come to you with their problems, you want to ease their burden and solve the issues at hand. But what people really need is for you to listen. Often, you try to solve their problems in order to relieve your own discomfort. Instead, you can help them to solve their own problems if you can guide them with authentic questions.

Palmer says that open and honest questions help "hear the other person into speech." Here are his seven guidelines:

Open and Honest Questions

1. **The best mark of an open, honest question is that you cannot anticipate the answer.** For example, you might ask questions like, "What was easy?" or "What was difficult?" You might ask, "What surprised you?" or "What did you learn?"

2. **Stay with the person's language.** Perhaps the person said she found herself in an "impossible situation." You might respond, "You said this was an impossible situation. Could you say more about what that means to you?"

3. **Ask questions related to the person, not just the problem.** You might ask things like, "What brings you joy?" or "What would a great day look like for you?"

4. **Trust your intuition.** Listen deeply and allow questions to come from your heart, not your head.

5. **Ask open-ended questions.** Yes/no questions don't get the person to open or expand their thinking.

6. **Ask questions aimed at helping the person rather than satisfying your curiosity.**

7. **Offer images or metaphors that might engage the person's imagination.** For example, you might ask something like, "If you were writing a book about this experience, what title might you give the book? What might you name this chapter?"

As you go through this week, try to truly listen to others, whether at home, the coffee shop, or the office. Ask open and honest questions whenever appropriate, and take notes on your experiences.

Response Practice Questions

This week, we introduced the concept of asking open and honest questions. Please consider and answer the following questions about your experience.

1. What was it like to listen to the other person speak and not start formulating a response before they had finished? What, if anything, helped you listen more deeply to the other person?

2. What was easy about not trying to "solve" the other person's problems? What was difficult?

3. When you stayed with the other person's language, what shift did you notice in the other person? In yourself? Please explain.

4. As you asked questions related to the person, not just the problem, what surprised you about the responses? In what ways did your understanding or appreciation of the other person change?

5. What did it feel like to ask questions from your heart as opposed to your head? In what ways were questions from your heart different from those you might have asked from your head?

Discussion Questions

In this unit, you focused on extending kindness to others in two ways: through the practice of metta and through asking open and honest questions. You've had an opportunity to reflect upon your experience with these practices on your own. Now you have a chance to engage with others, using the following questions to get the discussion started.

1. In what ways did you find yourself growing larger after practicing metta? In what ways did you find yourself getting smaller after practicing metta?

2. During your metta meditation, you extended kindness to people you find difficult or with whom you've experienced conflict. In what ways, if at all, did your practice change the way you feel about those people? The ways you interact with them?

3. Your meditation also had you extend kindness to all beings without exception, whether it was the drugstore cashier or the neighbor's cat. What did you feel inside after extending kindness to all beings?

4. When asking open and honest questions, what changes, if any, did you notice in the other person as your conversation progressed? What changes, if any, did you notice in yourself? What surprised you?

5. If you tried offering images or metaphors that might engage the other person's imagination, what did you observe about how that affected the other person? Did any insights emerge? How did offering images to others affect your own thinking?

This Week's Practices

☐ *Meditative practice—10 to 20 minutes per day:*
Metta.

☐ *Daily-life practice—each day:*
Metta on the spot.

☐ *Response practice—each day:*
Ask open and honest questions using Parker Palmer's guidelines.

☐ *Reflection—15 to 30 minutes at the end of the week:*
Choose one or more questions from the Meditative Practice and Daily-Life Practice Questions, Response Practice Questions, or Discussion Questions above, and write about your experience.

I Extend Compassion

Introduction

Last week, you focused on kindness—one antidote to aversion—through your metta practice. You ran the experiment to see whether kindness can help you dissolve the apparent barriers between yourself and others.

This week, you'll focus on compassion. Compassion simply means sharing pain or "feeling with" someone else, and it is another way of dissolving barriers.

When you see others in pain, you can do two things to help them. One is to try to eliminate the source of the pain. Many of the factors that contribute to people's pain are, however, beyond your control, and that can limit your ability to help in this way.

You can also engage with the person in pain—in part through the kind of mindful, open listening you learned from Parker Palmer. There is a meditative practice that allows you to engage as well: a structured process from the Tibetan wisdom tradition called *tonglen*, in which you take in the pain of others—absorb, digest, metabolize, and transform it—and then send back a message of freedom, engagement, and positive regard.

Tonglen, one of the Gateways to Presence, addresses all three poisons of mind driving the Cycle of Reactivity: aversion, craving, and delusion. We have a natural aversion to sharing the pain or suffering of others. We often crave to hold onto our own peace, joy, and sense of wellbeing. And delusion can show up in thoughts like, *I'm not involved here* or *These aren't my people or my concerns.* In each case, we seek to preserve our ego identity and the apparent security we achieve by staying separate from others.

With practice, tonglen can change you and your relationships. Instead of resisting or turning away from another's pain, you will learn to take it in, transform it, and then offer ease and peace to the other person.

Like metta, tonglen is a meditative practice that you can also apply in daily life. This week, you'll do tonglen on the spot. When you encounter others in pain, you'll imagine taking it in, metabolizing it, transforming it, and then sending back a sense of stillness, freedom, peace, and wellbeing.

In addition, you'll continue your response practice work, this week engaging with the five levels of listening and responding to negative emotions developed by Robert Kegan and Lisa Lahey. This work will build on your experience with Parker Palmer's open and honest questions, giving you another way to engage in skillful speech.

Meditative Practice

In *The Green Mile* by Stephen King,[14] death row inmate John Coffey has a special gift. He's able to feel the pain of others, transform it, and then provide healing to those who suffer.

In similar fashion, tonglen invites you to embrace and absorb the suffering of others and then transform it and send it back as healing thoughts. Tonglen is a powerful and emotionally charged practice that serves as an antidote to craving, aversion, and delusion: you will confront rather than turn away from suffering, and you will release rather than cling to freedom and ease.

We learned tonglen from Joel and Michelle Levey, who spent time working with people at our company. We've adapted the version below from their book *Living in Balance: A Mindful Guide for Thriving in a Complex World*.[15]

As always, we suggest you play a recording of the meditation so you can focus on the practice instead of trying to read and meditate simultaneously. You can use a version of this meditation that we have prerecorded and made available at www.psm-handbook.com, or you can record yourself reading the meditation aloud.

You'll need to find a quiet place where you can be uninterrupted for about fifteen minutes to half an hour.

Adopt a comfortable position that allows you to be alert. It's okay to sit or stand; just make sure you are sitting or standing up straight. If you become sleepy or dull during this practice, try straightening your spine. If you find yourself becoming tense, try taking a deep breath and relaxing your jaw and shoulders on the out-breath.

14 Stephen King, *The Green Mile* (New York: Signet Books, 1996).

15 Joel and Michelle Levey, *Living in Balance: A Mindful Guide for Thriving in a Complex World* (Studio City: Divine Arts, 2014).

Once you're comfortably situated, take a deep breath, feeling the cool air filling your lungs. Feel the warm air rush out through your mouth on the exhalation. Take another deep breath, closing your eyes on the in-breath, feeling the cool air come in and the warm air go out.

Allow the area around your heart and chest to relax, open, and soften. Establish a clear sense of inner spaciousness, like a vast open sky. Imagine or feel yourself as completely open and clear inside. Pause and rest here until you can establish this feeling of open, clear, and unobstructed inner spaciousness. Sense or imagine this as a stainless dimension of deep inner strength, purity, and compassionate presence.

Then, in this clear and open heart center, imagine a transformational vortex. You might visualize this as a fire of wisdom burning away the dross of illusions; a chunk of coal that transforms into a brilliant diamond; a crystalline matrix; or any other metaphor of transformation that suggests itself to you. This vortex is where you can draw in the smoke of the suffering of the world and turn it into the pure light of radiant compassion and wellbeing.

When you are ready, scan yourself for any pain or negativity that might be present in your physical, feeling, or thinking presence. Motivated by compassion—the desire to embrace, reduce or resolve suffering—as you inhale, imagine drawing any of these negative energies or potentialities into this pure dimension of the heart and, just as the darkness in a room disappears completely and immediately the moment the light switch is turned on, sense or imagine that any pain, suffering, or negativity is completely dissolved, resolved, and transformed. Breathing in heat or the fire of suffering and pain, let it dissolve into this pure dimension of your heart; sense that the suffering is completely dissolved and resolved; and then ride the waves of the out-breath to radiate compassion, comfort, and ease back to where the suffering came from.

As you exhale, imagine that from your heart center waves of clear, radiant, healing light pour forth. Imagine these waves filling your whole body and mind, healing, energizing, and transforming you. Allow the vortex at your heart to function as an energy transformer drawing in negativity, darkness, or pain, and transforming it into radiant light and healing energy.

Continue in this way, embracing, gathering, sweeping and vacuuming, resolving and transforming, mounted on the waves of the breath, for as long as you like. Remember to keep your breathing gentle and natural, not forcing or holding the breath in any way.

As you deepen in this practice, you realize that just as you wish to be free of the pain in your body, your loneliness, or heartache, so too does the person in the seat or house, the office, village, or country next to you, or across the world. And you also realize that it really doesn't take any extra effort at all as you breathe in to hold the compassionate intention to embrace and transform their suffering at the same time as you're breathing in and transforming your own.

If you are tormented by anger or grief, imagine and affirm that with each breath, as your compassion transforms these energies or feelings within the sphere of your own personal, local body or mind, those same feelings shared by others can be embraced and transformed by your compassion as well. Envision and affirm that the radiance of this compassion emanates out through you to be received by anyone who shares the same feelings, who suffers in the same way, or who even has the potential for such vulnerability in the future. Whatever the form of distress or suffering you find within yourself, embrace that in others or in the world at large. Mounted on the waves of the breath, receive and transform this discord with your heart of compassion and affirm the universality of your humanity and your kinship and heartfelt relationship to countless other beings who might share the same feelings, vulnerabilities, or concerns.

When it feels natural, allow the circle of your compassion to widen to embrace anyone else who comes to mind: a friend or loved one, a neighbor or coworker, a whole group of people who are living with fear, suffering, or danger. Breathing in, allow your heart to open, to touch, receive, embrace, and transform the fear, the distress, the loneliness, grief, or suffering. Allow these sorrows or distresses to dissolve and resolve completely within the pure, open, limitless dimension of your heart.

As this transformation naturally unfolds, allow the energy of your heartfelt compassion to dissolve or explode the delusion of separateness and expand your sense of identity into the larger field of being that includes all life. As you feel the sensations of your out-breath, allow your heart to naturally open to send back waves of peace, patience, calm, protection, lovingkindness, and radiant compassion to all who suffer. Experience the openness and connectedness that awaken as you expand the circle of your active, engaged compassion and caring in this way.

Continue to deepen into this meditation for as long as you like or have time for, allowing each cycle of breaths to further deepen and affirm your capacity to open your heart and expand the circle of your compassion.

This meditation can be done for many different situations. First, start with yourself, then let the circle of your compassionate awareness reach out to others yearning for the same quality of peace, harmony, and wellbeing that you're looking for, and keep expanding the circle of your compassion to individuals, groups, or other living beings who come to mind.

Daily-Life Practice

You come to a stop at a traffic light and see a dirty, disheveled man with the cardboard sign: "Vet. Anything helps. God bless." You don't have any money or fresh water bottles to give him.

As you're walking to the conference room for an important client meeting, you see a colleague take a deep breath and briefly put her head in her hands. You don't have time to stop.

In both cases—even if your mind isn't poisoned by aversion (*gross, I don't want to touch him*) and delusion (*not my problem*)—you may feel as though there's nothing you can do.

The good news is that when we encounter someone in pain, we can always practice tonglen. We can breathe in people's pain, transform it, and privately send them a sense of stillness, freedom, and peace.

This week, whenever you see someone in pain—whether a stranger, a loved one, or an acquaintance—silently absorb the pain you see, transform it within yourself, and then send the person healing thoughts of stillness and peace.

Meditative Practice and Daily-Life Practice Questions

In this unit, tonglen served as both your meditative practice and your daily-life practice. While meditating, you thought about someone in pain, absorbed it, transformed it, and then sent the person healing thoughts. Likewise, when you encountered suffering in daily life, you sought to take in the pain and replace it with healing.

Please consider and answer the following questions about your experience with tonglen, both in the context of the meditative practice and in that of the daily-life practice.

1. Last week in your metta practice, you wished others safety, happiness, health, and ease. This week, you confronted suffering, brought it into yourself, and radiated healing thoughts. Which of these practices resonated with you more strongly than the other? Why do you think that is?

2. It makes sense to feel skeptical that doing tonglen can by itself heal others' pain. Even if that's the case, in what other ways might tonglen be useful?

3. In what ways did tonglen practice affect your own pain?

4. How did practicing tonglen change the way you think about others? About yourself?

5. After you began your tonglen practice, what changes did you notice in your interactions with others?

Response Practice

You've learned that the practice of skillful speech is one of the Gateways to Presence. And you've seen that you cannot speak skillfully unless you listen consciously. In the last unit, you explored the practice of open and honest questions, which is built upon effective listening.

This week, we explore what Robert Kegan and Lisa Lahey call the five levels of listening and responding to negative emotions. Lahey is a professor at Harvard University's Graduate School of Education, as was Kegan for more than forty years. They divide listening into five levels that range from well-intentioned but misguided to fully engaged and empathetic.

Let's say you arrive at an important workshop, and a colleague mentions she is scared to make her presentation in front of so many senior managers. "Oh, you'll do great. You always do," you reply. Your intentions are solid; you want to help her. But what you're really saying is, "Don't feel the way you do."

This sort of response falls into **Level 1 Listening and Responding**. Although motivated by a sincere desire to help others and ease their anxiety, it **discounts their feelings** and doesn't allow you to meet them where they are.

In **Level 2 Listening and Responding**, you immediately **leap to finding a solution**. In the example above, you might say something like, "Just look at me during the presentation, and it'll be like we're having a regular conversation." Although there's certainly a place for problem-solving, Level 2 listening and responding doesn't allow you to express your humanity or to let the other person feel it. It's far better first to join in the other person's experience (see Level 4, below). Then you may be able to solve the problem together.

As Kegan and Lahey observe, one of the most precious experiences anyone can have is to know that someone is with you, that someone understands what you're feeling.

In **Level 3 Listening and Responding**, you **ask neutral questions**. Often, this is because you are trying to gain additional information so, again, you can solve the problem for the other person. For example, in our scenario about the worrisome presentation, you might ask, "Who are you worried about?" or "Do you know what their expectations are?" The problem with Level 3 listening and responding is that you're still not joining the other person where they are.

In **Level 4 Listening and Responding**, you **join in the specific emotion or concern being expressed**. In the case of your colleague with the presentation worries, that might be a feeling of anxiety. "It's really hard to speak in front of a high-powered group," you might say. This kind of response is filled with empathy; the other person knows you understand what he or she is experiencing. Empathy is to be contrasted with sympathy. In a sympathetic comment, you might say, "I feel bad for you," or "I'd hate that, too." The problem with sympathy is that it revolves around *you*, whereas empathy is about joining the other person's feelings.

Kegan and Lahey make an important point about Level 4 responses. You want to avoid providing a Level 4 response and then following it up with responses from Levels 1 to 3. If you do that, the other person may hear only the lower-level responses. But if you provide a Level 4 response, the other person may come to you later with a direct request for advice.

Finally, in **Level 5 Listening and Responding**, you **join the larger "feeling world" behind what the other person is saying**. In our presentation scenario, you might say, "I know how important it is to you to make a good impression with the senior managers and how hard you work on your presentations." By doing this, you join the person in their experience of having the problem so that, if they ask for your help, you can then find a solution to it together.

As you go through this week, try to listen and respond at Levels 4 and 5. Take notes on your experiences.

Response Practice Questions

For this unit's response practice, you studied Robert Kegan and Lisa Lahey's five levels of listening and responding to negative emotions. You also sought to implement their teachings as you went through the week, focusing on listening and responding at Levels 4 and 5.

To help you reflect on your experience with this practice, please consider and answer the following questions.

1. Under what circumstances did you notice yourself listening and responding to others at Levels 1 to 3 this week? Did this occur more often than you expected? What did you notice about those interactions?

2. Under what circumstances did you notice others responding to you at Levels 1 to 3 this week? How did that make you feel?

3. If you were able to engage with others at Levels 4 and 5, in what ways did that change your interactions with them?

4. When you engaged with them at Levels 4 and 5, what effects did you notice on the behavior and mood of others?

5. Feeling empathy and joining the "feeling world" behind what others are saying implies that you're sharing the burdens of others. In your experience with this practice, how were you affected when you shared these burdens? Did you feel heavier? Lighter? The same as usual?

Discussion Questions

In this week's unit, you adopted tonglen as both your meditative practice and your daily-life practice. You also studied and sought to implement the five levels of listening and responding to negative emotions. You've reflected on your experience with these practices on your own. Now you have an opportunity to further reflect with others, using the following questions to get you started.

1. In *The Green Mile*, John Coffey's gift of being able to feel the pain of others and heal it proved to be a terrific burden for him. In what ways did you find that practicing tonglen was difficult for you emotionally?

2. How did your feelings and attitudes about people change as you practiced tonglen? If your feelings and attitudes did not change, what did the absence of change feel like?

3. Both tonglen and the listening and responding practice rest on empathy—feeling what others are experiencing. How did you notice these practices breaking down the barriers between yourself and others? What did that feel like? If the barriers remained strong for you, what did that feel like?

4. As you engaged in your response practice, what shifts in your interactions with others did you notice? Did you feel closer to them? More separate from them?

5. Which of these practices would you most like to explore further? To continue practicing? Why?

This Week's Practices

☐ *Meditative practice—10 to 20 minutes per day:*
Tonglen.

☐ *Daily-life practice—each day:*
Tonglen on the spot.

☐ *Response practice—each day:*
When you encounter someone experiencing difficult emotions, practice listening and responding at Levels 4 and 5.

☐ *Reflection—15 to 30 minutes at the end of the week:*
Choose one or more questions from the Meditative and Daily-Life Practice Questions, Response Practice Questions, or Discussion Questions above, and write about your experience.

I Respond

Introduction

One of your direct reports is giving you a project update. At one point, he says, "The original supplier notified us he couldn't get us our order until next week, but . . ."

You jump in. "Unacceptable. We'll be off schedule and in breach of contract. We need that order."

If you had let your colleague finish, you would have learned that he'd arranged to get an on-time order from a different supplier at the same cost.

In previous weeks, you learned about the importance of conscious listening and did some exercises to help with the practice. This week, we introduce two additional approaches to skillful speech. You'll see that you can use them to communicate authentically, even when confronting difficult issues. With enough practice, you can internalize the guidelines so that the ability to speak skillfully becomes part of who you are.

First on the list? Always take a breath before speaking. Doing so keeps you from interrupting others and allows them to say all that they need to say—which would have saved you some anxiety in the interaction with the colleague and his bad news about the supplier.

Your meditative practice will be to combine a practice developed by Shinzen Young with Ken McLeod's Opening Practice. We'll call it the Core Opening Practice. It is meant to put you in touch with all aspects of your experience.

For your daily-life practice this week, you'll consider the practices that have been most helpful to you and build one you can use as a touchstone in your life.

Meditative Practice

The meditative practice this week invites you to get in touch with all aspects of your experience.

As you learned earlier, Shinzen's practices allow you to take internal talk, mental images, and body sensations (both physiological and emotional), all of which you normally consider part of yourself, and to hold them up to examination—in other words, to take up what you usually consider subject and make it object.

McLeod's Opening Practice encourages you to experience everything at once, to open your heart to it all, and to ask, "Who or what experiences this?"

As you saw in part 1 of this handbook, there are internal feelings (or emotions) and external feelings (or body sensations). For this meditation, as you notice the emotions, you will label them "feel in," and as you notice the physiological sensations, you will label them "feel out."

If you become aware of anger, sadness, or joy, you'll use the label "feel in." If you notice aches, pains, itches, etc., you'll label them "feel out." And rather than simply waiting for what shows up in awareness, you can direct your attention to one category and then to the other. You might begin by saying to yourself, "feel in," and then notice whether there are any emotions present. Then you can say, "feel out," and look for body sensations.

Next, you will turn your attention to seeing. The direction "see in" will point you to mental imagery. You will say to yourself, "see in," and then rest your awareness on your internal mental screen, noting whether there are images—clear, subtle, or none at all. Then you will say to yourself, "see out," and note what images come from the external world.

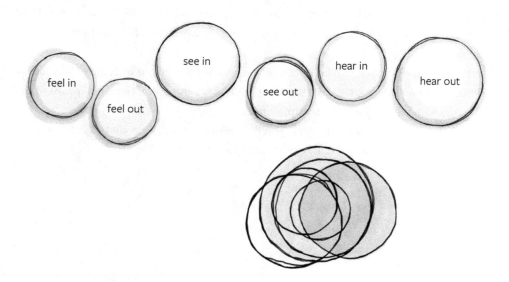

Finally, you will turn to hearing. Saying to yourself, "hear in," you will rest your attention at talk home base and listen for internal words, phrases, or subtle stirrings. Turning to "hear out," you will note sounds coming from the external environment.

There are three forms of awareness—feeling, seeing, and hearing—and two modalities—internal and external. The result is six categories and six instructions to yourself: "feel in," "feel out," "see in," "see out," "hear in," and "hear out."

As always, we suggest you play a recording of the meditation so you can focus on the practice instead of trying to read and meditate simultaneously. You can use a version of this meditation that we have prerecorded and made available at www.psm-handbook.com, or you can record yourself reading the meditation aloud.

Find a quiet place where you can be uninterrupted for about fifteen to twenty minutes.

Please adopt a comfortable position that allows you to be alert. If you sit, make sure you're sitting up straight. If during the practice you become sleepy or dull, try straightening your spine or standing up. If you become tense, try taking a deep breath and relaxing your shoulders on the out-breath. **For this practice, it is best to leave your eyes open.**

Take a deep breath, feeling the cool air coming in through your nostrils and the warm air rushing out through your mouth. Take another deep breath, leaving your eyes open on the out-breath. Breathing normally, bring your attention to your body.

Think to yourself or say out loud the words "feel in," and notice what emotions are present for you. Stay with this for a few breaths.

Think to yourself or say aloud the words "feel out," and pay attention to the body sensations you are experiencing. There is no need to judge or change anything, only to notice.

Next, shift your awareness to your internal mental screen, and see what images become clearly visible or subtly visible as you think or speak the words "see in." If no images appear for you, take note.

Shift now to the visual world outside of you. Think or speak the words "see out" and notice what visually presents itself to your attention.

Next, turn your attention to your talk home base and think to yourself, or say to yourself, "hear in." Notice what internal words, phrases, or subtle stirrings are present for you.

Now shift your attention to the world outside of your body as you think to yourself or speak the words "hear out." What sounds around you come into your awareness?

Now that you've gone through all six categories, "free-float" among them, turning your attention to whichever is most prominent at that moment. You can simply note them, or you can label to yourself each as it arises.

Finally, layer one category on top of the other and open to all six at the same time. Open your heart to all you experience.

With your heart open, and your awareness on all six categories, consider the question: "Who or what experiences all this?"

There is no need to answer the question. Simply rest in the shift you may experience.

Return to noting the six categories—beginning with one at a time.

Feel in.

Feel out.

See in.

See out.

Hear in.

Hear out.

Then, again, hold all six in your mind and your heart as you ask, "Who or what experiences all this?"

Repeat this process for as long as you like—exploring each of the six categories one at a time, then holding them all in your awareness with an open heart, then asking, "Who or what experiences all this?"

Take a deep breath, feeling the cool air come in through your nose and the warmth of your exhalation rushing from your mouth.

We think this is a good meditative practice with which to conclude because in a sense it covers everything, all six modes of your experience. If you were to choose one meditative practice to carry forward into the coming weeks and months, this might be it.

Daily-Life Practice

When you began the Practice of Self-Management, your first daily-life practice was to **note knee-jerk reactions**. As you progressed, you refined your attention, successively noting the internal words and mental images, body sensations, and emotions that arise when knee-jerk reactions occur.

After building your awareness of how often you experience knee-jerk reactions and what happens within you when they occur, you moved on to examining some of the **underlying causes of your knee-jerk reactions**, like arguing with what is. For example, perhaps you found yourself behind schedule on a project. When you realized you were not going to meet your deadline, you might have said to yourself something like, *We shouldn't be behind on this project*. Your practice was to remind yourself, "But we are."

Later you built on that practice, **not only accepting what is but saying "yes" to it as though you'd chosen it**.

You eventually shifted your focus from your knee-jerk reactions and placed it on **being kind and empathetic**. You practiced **metta** on the spot, wishing those you saw—from loved ones to strangers to difficult coworkers—safety, happiness, health, and ease.

You followed your metta practice with **tonglen**. When you encountered someone in pain, you sought to absorb it, transform it, and send back to that person a sense of freedom and peace.

Now it's time to reflect on which daily-life practices were most helpful to you and to create your own set of practices to use as touchstones in your life.

For example, perhaps monitoring your body when you're triggered to reactivity has helped you slow down and avoid knee-jerk reactions. Or maybe you've found the practice of saying "yes" to what is has helped bring you into alignment with reality.

If several of our practices have proved useful, you could create a hybrid practice. For example, imagine seeing a homeless person begging along a street median. *I wish so many people weren't in such need*, you might think. But then you might follow that thought up with, "But they are." Then you could silently say, "May you be free from danger. May you be happy. May you be healthy. May you live with ease." In this scenario, you've combined saying "yes" to what is with your practice of metta.

There is no wrong practice. Choose something you'll stick with that is valuable and helpful to you.

Meditative Practice and Daily-Life Practice Questions

For this unit's meditative practice, you combined Shinzen Young's practice with Ken McLeod's Opening Practice as a way of helping you get in touch with all aspects of your experience. We called this new practice the Core Opening Practice.

For your daily-life practice this week, you built your own set of practices based upon those you've encountered in this handbook.

Please use the questions below to reflect on your experience with these practices.

1. In the Core Opening Practice, you first checked in with what was happening in various parts of your body and mind, one at a time. What did you notice? What similarities did you discover between seeing "in" and seeing "out"? Feeling "in" and feeling "out"? Hearing "in" and hearing "out"? When you "free-floated" among the experiences—i.e., noted the most prominent—what did you notice?

2. In the second part of the Core Opening Practice, you were invited to experience at the same time all that was going on in your body and mind. What was that experience like for you? How did the practice affect your sense of what happens within you all the time?

3. In the third part of the Core Opening Practice, you were invited to ask but not answer the question, "Who or what experiences all of this?" Now that you've had multiple experiences with this practice, how would you answer that question?

4. For the daily-life practice, you were invited to build your own set of practices to use as touchstones in your life. What factors did you consider in deciding which practice or practices to choose? Why those factors?

5. In what ways have the practices you chose been helpful?

Response Practice

You've seen it time and time again: a politician or other public figure says something controversial and within a day or so issues an apology along the lines of, "I'm sorry if anyone was offended." Most of us, whether we were offended or not, don't consider that a real apology. That's because this kind of apology isn't "real speech"—that is, it is not an example of skillful speech.

According to some teachers, skillful speech has five qualities: it is **timely, truthful, kind, gentle, and beneficial**. People find it useful to remember these qualities by their initial letters, **TTKGB**. (We know what you're thinking—you'd need a mnemonic to remember that mnemonic! It works best if you say it out loud. Try it. In our fifteen years of teaching, we've found the letters quickly become second nature and help people respond appropriately.)

In the example above, a politician using skillful speech might say something like, "I spoke without thinking, and my comment hurt many people. I am sorry for having made it. I learned from this and will do better in the future."

As an alternative or complement to TTKGB, you can think of skillful speech as having the qualities Ken McLeod ascribes to it: it is accurate, relevant, constructive, and draws in the listener.

Imagine you're meeting a new hire for lunch. You'll be working with this person closely on a big project. As you wait for your meal, you ask questions like, "Do you like this city?" Asking closed-ended questions like this invites only simple facts or else "yes" or "no" responses. It's no wonder you leave lunch feeling as though you still barely know your new coworker. But if you engage in skillful speech, you might end lunch with a much deeper appreciation of your colleague.

If skillful speech—real speech—is so important, how can you practice it?

McLeod has drawn up a list of five guidelines he believes are helpful in speaking skillfully.

Ken McLeod's Guidelines for Skillful Speech

1. **Take a breath before saying anything. Always.** For one thing, that breath creates a pause in your speech that reduces the chance you will interrupt others. It also provides a greater chance that others will have a full opportunity to say what they need to say and to say it completely. Just as important, taking a breath increases the chance that people will listen to what you have to say instead of feeling resentful that you cut them off.

2. **When you speak, listen to your own voice as if you were listening to another person.** When you listen to yourself as though someone else were speaking, you're much more alive to shifts in tone that can undercut or confuse your message. You might realize and think to yourself, *Oh my. Even though I'm talking about how our profits have risen, my voice sounds edgy, like I have an axe to grind.* Or you may realize you're using the same phrase over and over, reducing the power of your speech. McLeod believes that even just a few days of this practice will help you better appreciate the clear, powerful resonance of real speech.

3. **Ask open questions.** Open, or open-ended, questions invite others to express their views and ideas rather than simple facts or a quick "yes" or "no." Of course, there is a time and a place for closed-ended questions. A 9-1-1 operator is not denying the caller's humanity by asking, "Is the patient conscious?" But there are many other times when asking open-ended questions is more important—and revealing. In our example above, you might say, "What's surprised you about this city?" or "How does this city compare with where you used to live?"

4. **When you apologize, apologize for your actions, not for the results.** This is a good example of real speech. Name and take responsibility for your action. "I'm sorry if I offended you" is not a real apology. "I'm sorry that I called you a monster" is a real apology. You can't always know the results of your actions, whether fortunate or not. An apology—a real apology—is not contingent on the results of your action. It's about the action itself.

5. **Be impeccable with your word.** How you talk with others directly shapes your relationships with them. When you say what you mean and mean what you say, you inspire trust and confidence. Others take you seriously. Please note that this also applies to how you speak to yourself. Too often, you don't use a real voice with yourself, instead using the voice of those who have criticized or built you up to make use of you for their own needs. Real speech is just as important internally as it is externally. Sometimes you tell yourself "small" lies, perhaps exaggerating your contributions or rationalizing your actions. These may spring from a fear that you are not good enough—another lie. It's important to speak honestly, always, whether with others or with yourself.

As you go through this week, seek to engage in skillful speech using McLeod's guidelines or the rubric **TTKGB: Timely, Truthful, Kind, Gentle, and Beneficial.** Some people find it useful to write these attributes on a yellow sticky note and place it near their office telephone. Bear in mind that skillful speech is not possible without conscious listening. Take notes on how practicing skillful speech shapes and changes your relationships with others.

Response Practice Questions

In this unit, you learned two more approaches to skillful speech: TTKBG and Ken McLeod's guidelines for speaking skillfully. His guidelines are: take a breath before speaking; listen to your own voice as though it belonged to someone else; ask open-ended questions; apologize for your actions, not the results of your actions; and be impeccable with your word.

Reflecting upon your experience with speaking skillfully, please consider and answer the following questions.

1. In what ways did McLeod's guidelines differ from your previous practice? In what ways were they what you already strive to do?

2. Many people dislike hearing recordings of their voices. How was your experience of listening to your voice as you spoke? In what ways was this practice helpful to you?

3. What was your experience of taking a breath before speaking? Under what circumstances did this practice save you embarrassment or misunderstanding?

4. What did it feel like when you caught yourself asking closed-ended questions? How did your experience shift when you asked open-ended questions?

5. Which of the guidelines did you find most useful in promoting skillful speech, and why?

Discussion Questions

In this unit, we introduced as your meditative practice the Core Opening Practice, a combination of Shinzen's practice and McLeod's Opening Practice, and we introduced two additional approaches to the practice of skillful speech. You also selected and employed one or more of the daily-life practices from previous units. You've had the opportunity to ponder your experience with these practices privately. Here are questions you can reflect on in a group.

1. During the Core Opening Practice, you first noted each of the six modalities in turn (feel in, feel out, see in, see out, hear in, hear out), and then you free-floated, noting which was most prominent and then moving onto the next; second, you attempted to hold in awareness all six modalities simultaneously; third, you asked, "Who or what experiences all this?" and rested in the shift that may have occurred. Why were some of the phrases easier? Why were some more difficult?

2. In what ways did your sense of yourself change during and after your experience with the Core Opening Practice? How has that different sense of self remained with you?

3. You learned that skillful speech is timely, truthful, kind, gentle, and beneficial (TTKGB). Ken McLeod defines it as accurate, relevant, drawing the listener in, and constructive. How did these descriptions help you implement this practice?

4. Among McLeod's five guidelines for skillful speech is a note on apologies. He urges that when you apologize, you apologize for your actions, not the result of those actions. Why is apologizing for results—the impact of our actions—not skillful speech?

5. Another of McLeod's guidelines stresses the importance of being "impeccable with your word." While you understand you wouldn't want to say you'll finish a project by tomorrow if you know it will be impossible to complete until next week, how can you be truly impeccable with your word when unforeseen events could derail your promises? What would skillful speech have you do and say under these circumstances?

This Week's Practices

☐ *Meditative practice—10 to 20 minutes per day:*
Core Opening Practice.

☐ *Daily-life practice—each day:*
Your choice.

☐ *Response practice—each day:*
Engage in Ken McCleod's five guidelines or TTKGB in order to continue your ability to practice skillful speech (begun with Parker Palmer's open and honest questions as well as Kegan and Lahey's five levels of listening and responding to negative emotions).

☐ *Reflection—15 to 30 minutes at the end of the week:*
Choose one or more questions from the Meditative and Daily-Life Practice Questions, Response Practice Questions, or Discussion Questions above, and write about your experience.

Conclusion

In this handbook we've introduced a number of concepts and practices whose purpose is:

1. to reduce reactivity and foster appropriate responses by helping you turn subject into object;

2. to encourage presence; and

3. to dissolve the apparent barriers between yourself and others.

Our hope is that these practices have opened new worlds and experiences for you. You expanded your awareness by taking note of your knee-jerk reactions and the internal states that accompany them. Along the way, you gained an understanding of how assumptions about the way the world is or should be generate reactivity, and you learned how to inquire into what is really true. By the end of the program, your practice included metta, tonglen, and skillful speech—practices that dissolve the barriers between you and others through kindness and compassion.

Each of the three parts of this handbook introduced you to entire worlds of which many people are unaware. The first part explored thinking, feeling, imagery, and sensation—an inner world unexplored by most of us but vital to pursuing the question, "Who am I?" In part 2, you saw a world of "shoulds," "shouldn'ts," and stories we accept as true without much curiosity or inquiry. This sets up a competition between what is actually happening and what we think and want to be happening. And as Byron Katie says, suffering comes from arguing with reality.

The third part of the book then took you deeper into your interconnectedness—your inter-being—through kindness and compassion. This, too, is a new world, one in which you realized that you are not separate, alone, and disconnected, but part of something that connects us all.

This handbook is drawing to a conclusion. But in a very real way, your opportunity is just beginning.

In the last unit, you took the first steps toward **creating your own daily-life practices** based upon those introduced throughout this program. If you stay with them, new worlds will continue to open.

You'll also benefit from **continuing with a regular meditative practice**. Select a practice that has proved helpful to you and adjust when needed. Perhaps the Core Opening Practice is best for you now, but six months from now you might find that tonglen would prove most beneficial.

Also continue **returning to and re-reading the material**, particularly the questions in each unit. You may be surprised to see how your understanding deepens and grows with further experience and practice.

By continuing practices that promote presence, you'll be able to more quickly sense when you are becoming reactive. Over time, you will be better equipped to recognize and challenge the beliefs and assumptions that give rise to reactivity. And by engaging in practices that promote empathy and kindness, you'll be able to see the human being beneath the reactivity in your coworkers, customers, or strangers—people who are more than the stories you create about them, people who want the same things in life that you do.

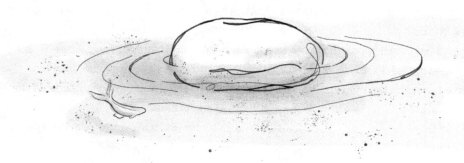

Bibliography

Durant, Will. *The Story of Philosophy: The Lives and Opinions of the World's Greatest Philosophers.* New York: Pocket Books, 1991.

Hanh, Thich Nhat. *Peace Is Every Step.* New York: Bantam Books, 1992.

Hemingway, Ernest. "Monologue to the Maestro: A High Seas Letter." In *By-Line Ernest Hemingway: Selected Articles and Dispatches of Four Decades*, edited by William White, 213–20. New York: Charles Scribner's Sons, 1967.

Katie, Byron. "Judge-Your-Neighbor Worksheet." *The Work of Byron Katie.* https://thework.com/wp-content/uploads/2019/02/jyn_en_mod_6feb2019_r4_form1.pdf.

———. *Loving What Is: Four Questions That Can Change Your Life.* In collaboration with Stephen Mitchell. New York: Harmony Books, 2002.

———. "The Work Is a Practice." *The Work of Byron Katie.* http://thework.com/sites/thework /downloads/worksheets/instructions_for_thework.pdf.

———. "The Work of Byron Katie: An Introduction." *The Work of Byron Katie.* https://thework.com/wp-content/uploads/2019/02/English_LB.pdf.

King, Stephen. *The Green Mile.* New York: Signet Books, 1996.

Kofman, Fred. "Be a Player, Not a Victim – LinkedIn Speaker Series." YouTube video, 12:56. August 12, 2013. https://www.youtube.com/watch?v=xXdN5kMioRQ.

———. *Conscious Business: How to Build Value through Values.* Louisville, CO: Sounds True, 2006. CD-ROM. (Audio download through https://www.soundstrue.com/store/conscious -business-4036.html.)

———. *Conscious Business: How to Build Value through Values.* Louisville, CO: Sounds True, 2013.

Levey, Joel and Michelle. *Living in Balance: A Mindful Guide for Thriving in a Complex World.* Studio City: Divine Arts, 2014.

Loori, John Daido. *Finding the Still Point: A Beginner's Guide to Zen Meditation.* Boston: Shambhala Publications, 2007.

McLeod, Ken. *An Arrow to the Heart: A Commentary on the Heart Sutra.* Bloomington, IN: Trafford Publishing, 2007.

———. *The Unfettered Mind: Pragmatic Buddhism.* http://unfetteredmind.org.

———. *Wake Up to Your Life: Discovering the Buddhist Path of Attention*. New York: HarperCollins, 2002.

Palmer, Parker J. *Center for Courage & Renewal*. www.couragerenewal.org/parker.

———. *A Hidden Wholeness: The Journey Toward an Undivided Life*. San Francisco: John Wiley & Sons, 2004.

Tolle, Eckhart. "Eckhart Tolle on the Radical State of Being." Talk presented at Bodhi Tree Bookstore, West Hollywood, CA, 1999. *Bodhi Tree*. https://bodhitree.com/journal /archives-eckhart-tolle-state-of-being/.

———. *The Power of Now: A Guide to Spiritual Enlightenment*. Novato, CA: New World Library, 1999.

———. *Stillness Speaks*. Vancouver: Namaste Publishing, 2003.

Wallace, David Foster. "This Is Water." YouTube, 22:43, from a commencement speech to Kenyon College class of 2005. Posted by Jamie Sullivan, May 19, 2013. https://www.youtube.com/watch?v=8CrOL-ydFMI.

Wilber, Ken. Foreword to *Coming Home: The Experience of Enlightenment in Sacred Traditions*, by Lex Hixon, vii–x. Burdett, NY: Larson Publications, 1995.

Young, Shinzen. *Shinzen Young*. http://www.shinzen.org.

———. *Unified Mindfulness*. http://www.unifiedmindfulness.com.

Further Reading

Burkeman, Oliver. *The Antidote: Happiness for People Who Can't Stand Positive Thinking.* New York: Farrar, Straus and Giroux, 2013.

Chödrön, Pema. *Living Beautifully with Uncertainty and Change.* Boston: Shambhala Publications, 2012.

———. *The Places That Scare You: A Guide to Fearlessness in Difficult Times.* Boston: Shambhala Publications, 2001.

Goldstein, Joseph. *Insight Meditation: The Practice of Freedom.* Boston: Shambhala Publications, 1993.

Hartong, Leo. *Awakening to the Dream: The Gift of Lucid Living.* Salisbury, UK: Non-Duality Press, 2001.

Salzberg, Sharon. *Lovingkindness: The Revolutionary Art of Happiness.* Boston: Shambhala Publications, 1995.

Suzuki, Shunryu. *Zen Mind, Beginner's Mind: Informal Talks on Zen Meditation and Practice.* New York: Weatherhill, 1970.

Watts, Alan W. *The Wisdom of Insecurity.* New York: Pantheon Books, 1951.

Christopher Forman
is CEO of the Decurion
Corporation and chairman of its
subsidiaries ArcLight Cinemas,
Pacific Theatres, and Robertson
Properties Group. He is cofounder
of Citizens of the World Charter
Schools and the Center for
Humanity. He received degrees
in history, philosophy, and
business from Harvard, Oxford,
and Stanford. He has practiced
Iyengar yoga and various forms
of Eastern and Western
meditation for more than
twenty years.

Bryan Ungard

is chief purpose officer of Decurion Management Company. He is accountable for the ways in which Decurion operates its businesses so there is no trade-off between excellent business and human flourishing. Bryan joined Decurion as its chief information officer. He received his bachelor's degree in computer science from Hiram College and his masters of business administration from the University of Michigan. Bryan holds a 2nd-Dan black belt in aikido.

ELEVATE HUMANITY THROUGH BUSINESS.

WE BELIEVE THAT BUSINESS IS GOOD BECAUSE IT CREATES VALUE, IT IS ETHICAL BECAUSE IT IS BASED ON VOLUNTARY EXCHANGE, IT IS NOBLE BECAUSE IT CAN ELEVATE OUR EXISTENCE, AND IT IS HEROIC BECAUSE IT LIFTS PEOPLE OUT OF POVERTY AND CREATES PROSPERITY. FREE ENTERPRISE CAPITALISM IS THE MOST POWERFUL SYSTEM FOR SOCIAL COOPERATION AND HUMAN PROGRESS EVER CONCEIVED. IT IS ONE OF THE MOST COMPELLING IDEAS WE HUMANS HAVE EVER HAD. BUT WE CAN ASPIRE TO EVEN MORE.

Excerpt from the Conscious Capitalist Credo. Read it in its entirety at www.consciouscapitalism.org/about/credo.

Conscious Capitalism is a paradigm that places people at the center of business. Conscious Capitalism, Inc. is an organization that brings businesses and business leaders on a conscious journey to elevate humanity through business by convening conscious capitalists, providing learning and development opportunities, and garnering PR for businesses, making the world a better place.

There are Conscious Capitalism events happening around the globe each week with over eighty conscious capitalist communities in twenty countries whose purpose is to connect with others, provide inspiration through storytelling, and give information and resources that allow community members to become stronger voices for business as a force for good.

We invite you, either as an individual or as a business, to get involved by joining us at a Conscious Capitalism event or a learning and development offering, and by sharing your story.

Learn more and join the movement at www.consciouscapitalism.org.

CPSIA information can be obtained
at www.ICGtesting.com
Printed in the USA
FSHW021124240919
62314FS